IMPERIAL KNIGHTS

HONOUR THROUGH FEALTY

CONTENTS

PRODUCED BY GAMES WORKSHOP IN NOTTINGHAM

With thanks to the Mournival and the Infinity Circuit for their additional playtesting services

Games Workshop Ltd, Willow Rd, Lenton, Nottingham, NG7 2WS
games-workshop.com

INTRODUCTION

Welcome, Noble pilot, to *Codex: Imperial Knights*. This tome is a comprehensive guide to the mighty war engines of the knightly households, from their terrifying weapons and ground-shaking battles of conquest to their magnificent heraldry and endless rolls of honour and victory. Read on, and prepare to sit the Throne Mechanicum!

Imperial Knights are a unique faction within Warhammer 40,000, for their armies typically comprise just a handful of models. Where other players' forces contain infantry, battle tanks, monstrous beasts and the like, an Imperial Knights army is made up solely of towering, heavily armed and armoured bipedal war engines. Even the least of these is more than a match for whole regiments of the foe. Piloted by highly trained Nobles whose minds are saturated with concepts of chivalry, honour and fealty, these ironclad giants shatter battle lines with ease, devastating the enemy's forces with bombardments of searing energy and explosive shells. Those who somehow survive this fusillade – and are not subsequently trampled underfoot – are sent scattering before the Knights like leaves on a gale.

There are many reasons to collect and play with an army of Imperial Knights. Quite aside from the heady thrill of directing an entire army of super-heavy war engines on the field of battle, there is the fact that every Knight is a modelling project in its own right. Large and incredibly detailed kits with a plethora of options and ample space for elaborately painted heraldry, Knights reward a collector who is willing to lavish attention on each model in turn. The payoff for this, of course, is that just a few of these towering miniatures makes up a potent tabletop army that looks absolutely spectacular, and poses a unique array of strategic challenges for both yourself and your opponent in every game of Warhammer 40,000.

Within this book you will find all the information you need to collect an Imperial Knights army and field it upon the tabletop.

WARRIORS OF THE NOBLE HOUSES: This section details the history of the Noble households, including their origins, allegiances and the wars they have fought against the Imperium's enemies.

IN ADAMANT CLAD: Here you will find a showcase of beautifully painted miniatures displaying the heraldry of the Imperial Knights, as well as example armies to inspire your own collection.

KNIGHTLY HOST: This section includes datasheets and weapon rules for every Imperial Knights unit for you to use in your games.

MIGHT OF THE KNIGHT WORLDS: This section provides additional rules – including Warlord Traits, Stratagems, Heirlooms of the Noble Houses and matched play points – that allow you to transform your collection of miniatures into an illustrious household of Imperial Knights.

To play games with your army, you will need a copy of the Warhammer 40,000 rules. To find out more about Warhammer 40,000 or download the free core rules, visit warhammer40000.com.

Before the gates of Hive Halathor, amidst the fire and fury of the War of Reaping, the Imperial Knights marched out to battle. They met the daemonic hordes of Chaos head on, their vox horns blaring proud hymns, their cannon fire a constant deafening thunder. Upon that fateful day it was honour, courage and nobility that prevailed over hatred and rage, and the Knights crushed the malefic fiends beneath their

WARRIORS OF THE NOBLE HOUSES

Imperial Knights are towering bipedal engines of war. Bristling with fearsome weapons and protected by shimmering ion fields, each piloted by a single elite Noble, Knights are amongst the most terrifying military assets in the entire Imperium.

The ground shakes as the Imperial Knights stride to battle. Mechanical giants that typically dominate their surrounding landscape, they cannot conceal their advance, nor would they – they know well the terror that their coming strikes into the hearts of the foe. Even amidst the smoke and grime of war, their heraldry shines out proudly for all to see: bright colours and magnificent designs tell of victories won and honours claimed, inspiring hope in their allies and dismay in foes.

Pistons and servo-motors hiss, whine and thump as they propel the Knights forwards with loping strides. Plasma reactors rumble. Exhaust vents cough black smoke into the skies as power floods through the Knights' armoured limbs. At the heart of each mighty war engine sits a Noble pilot, wired into their Throne Mechanicum and viewing the world through their steed's auspex feeds and data-manifolds. It is these accomplished warriors that direct the Knight suits in battle, and it is they who unleash their devastating weapons systems upon the luckless foe.

Even a single Knight can level enough firepower to obliterate infantry regiments or reduce armoured columns to smoking scrap. Ironstorm missiles streak from their launchers in trails of smoke to detonate amongst the enemy ranks, creating showers of gore. Avenger gatling cannons spin up to speed, screaming like a chorus of damned souls as they spray hundreds of thousands of rounds into their victims. Volcano lances spit streams of searing death, while thermal cannons reduce their targets to drifting ash. Corrupted fortifications tumble before the Knights' monstrous firepower, crashing down in billowing clouds of flame and rockcrete dust. Immense war machines and monstrous beasts alike are blasted limb from limb, while heretic hordes flee, their broken survivors clawing at one another in their desperation to escape the Knights' long shadows.

Even those who somehow weather the Knights' apocalyptic firepower have bought themselves only a temporary stay of execution. Now they must face the Knights at close

quarters, a prospect that none but the most insane would relish. From the whirring teeth of the enormous reaper chainsword to the crackling articulated wrecking ball that is the thunderstrike gauntlet, the Knights' melee armaments are more than capable of decapitating an Ork Gorkanaut or hurling a battle tank through the air like so much worthless junk. Furthermore, the sheer bulk of each Knight is a weapon in its own right: every thunderous footfall crushes armour, flesh and bone with the ease of an Imperial Guardsman stomping on a galley-roach.

The enemy's only chance is to level overwhelming destructive power against the Imperial Knights, hoping to bring them down through sheer weight of concentrated fire. Yet even the most destructive of projectiles may be deflected or robbed of their impact by the Knights' ion fields, and experienced Nobles have become expert at angling these shields to best effect. Solid shells and laser blasts splash against the ionic barriers in flares of blue-tinged light, the Knights marching on unperturbed and unharmed over earth left ravaged and burning by the enemy's futile attacks.

> *'Into them, lords and ladies! Into them! Let us purge these honourless vermin in the Emperor's name!'*
> – Sir Massimo of House Hawkshroud

A Knight is a fearsome opponent. Whether it be a swift Armiger, a stalwart Questor, or one of the indomitable constructs known as Dominus-class Knights, just one of these engines has the power to turn the tide of a battle. Yet when they deploy en masse, the knightly households possess the martial strength to conquer entire star systems in the Emperor's name. Led by Exalted Courts of high-ranking Barons, the Knights advance in lance formations, some acting as mobile gun platforms while others surge forward to carve and smash the foe apart at close quarters. Their tactics are typically swift and decisive: line-breaking charges, devastating flank attacks and punishing barrages leave the Knights' enemies scattered in disarray.

> *'Let the power of your Knight flow through your veins. Let the ghosts of your Throne whisper wisdom into your mind. Let steel be your sinews and fire be your fists. Become your Knight, as it becomes you, and through symbiosis ascend. So shall you Become. So shall you protect your people and slaughter your foes.'*
>
> – Sixth Canticle of the Ritual of Becoming

The manoeuvrability and speed of Imperial Knights is breathtaking to behold, far in excess of anything that such huge war machines should be able to achieve. Central to this remarkable agility and responsiveness is the unique neural bond that a Noble shares with his or her Knight. That, in turn, is thanks to the technologies of the Throne Mechanicum.

Each Throne is a testament to the incredible accomplishments of the Age of Technology, a pinnacle creation of a long forgotten era. These contraptions mount neural jacks and cerebral uplinks that connect directly to a Noble's cranial sockets, allowing them to interface with the Throne and, through it, the Knight into which it is reverently fitted. By linking their sensorium and nervous system to their Throne Mechanicum, a Noble can control the Knight suit as though it were an extension of their own body. Its mechanical senses become their own, its immense weaponry theirs to wield. For an unprepared mind, madness would swiftly follow. For a Noble of the knightly houses, conditioned since birth and cerebrally augmented to bear the neural load, it is ascension to virtual omnipotence.

Beyond their interface and control circuits, Thrones Mechanicum also contain mnemic engram reliquaries and spectrobionic foci that allow them to store the synaptic echoes of those with whom they bond. In short, each Throne is haunted by the ghosts of the pilots who came before. Many Nobles speak of whispering voices, visions and countless other strange manifestations that provide them with guidance and wisdom in battle.

The Throne Mechanicum does not just provide strategic advice. These ancient relics contain behavioural subroutines that weed out unworthy aspirants, and condition those who survive with notions of honour, chivalry and fealty. When a young Noble reaches their eighteenth year, they must undergo the Ritual of Becoming. They are led with great solemnity to their house's Sanctuary, a vast fortified structure within their ancestral stronghold that contains the Chamber of Echoes. Therein, they are connected to one of their house's dormant Thrones Mechanicum, enduring the cold stab of their neural jacks coupling for the first time. They are left, typically for a full night, alone in the dark with the ghosts of their Throne. The young aspirant must wrestle with the energies of the Throne Mechanicum, attempting to imprint their psyche upon it and withstand the receipt of its cerebral engrams in turn.

Sometimes this process is enough to drive the unfortunate aspirant quite mad. Others are killed outright, found as pale corpses whose cranial plugs still smoulder and whose features are twisted into ghastly masks of terror. Those who survive emerge forever changed, their childhood left behind and the mantle of knighthood resting heavy on their shoulders. It is no small sacrifice that these Nobles make for their power, yet it is one they make without the slightest hesitation.

THE KNIGHT WORLDS

The first Knight worlds were settled during the earliest epoch of human expansion into the stars. They weathered the Age of Strife, and were rediscovered and brought back into the fold during the golden era of the Great Crusade.

With each of these Knight worlds representing an exceptional concentration of martial strength, there was competition between the Imperial Administratum and the Cult Mechanicus to secure their allegiance. The Knight worlds of the modern Imperium thus have differing alignments. Those pledging loyalty to the Emperor are known as Questor Imperialis. They deal with the Adeptus Mechanicus only as much as they must to maintain their Knight suits. Others are sworn wholly to the service of the Omnissiah: these are Questor Mechanicus, and – while still fighting for the Imperium – they obey the diktats of Mars in all things. Those exiles of the knightly houses, and those who are the last of their Noble kin, are known as Freeblades. Such wandering mercenaries still fight for the Imperium, but may exhibit all manner of strange traits.

For all their differences, Imperial and Mechanicus-aligned Knight worlds share certain key aspects. All are ruled by one or more Noble houses, each of which owes fealty to their planet's overall ruler, typically a High Monarch or a Princeps. All maintain feudal systems of rulership that see the serf classes labour to support their knightly lords, who in turn defend their subjects from the predations of aliens, mutants and heretics. All are hidebound by layer upon layer of courtly protocols and interminable rituals that have built up like sediment over the millennia, and which the majority of Nobles will gladly go to war simply to escape. And, of course, though Knight worlds may occasionally fall prey to internecine wars of succession or duels of honour, they are all quick to march out to the aid of the wider Imperium in times of need.

Another unifying factor of all Knight worlds is the strange order of pseudo Tech-Priests known as Sacristans who maintain the Nobles' Knight suits. Trained by the Martian Priesthood and skilled in every aspect of knightly technology, these monastic orders devote their lives to ensuring that the Knights continue to fight. It speaks volumes about the martial pride of the Knight worlds that the Sacristans place as great a level of importance upon the heraldry and panoply of their titanic charges as they do upon keeping their power plants and weapons systems running. Thus it is not uncommon for a Knight to be seen after battle encased in servo-repair armatures and swarming with Sacristans, each lavishing as much time and care upon retouching the war machine's scarred paintwork as repairing more detrimental battle damage. By the tenets of the revered Code Chivalric, a Knight must not only be able to fight, but must look suitably magnificent while doing so.

Though their ways may seem strange and archaic to many within the Imperium, there can be no doubt that the Imperial Knights are powerful allies. With the coming of the Great Rift, their strength has never been more needed. From the bastion lines of the Segmentum Solar to the dark reaches of the Imperium Nihilus, and from the white-hot battlefronts of the Indomitus Crusade to the imperilled fringes of the Emperor's realm, the Imperial Knights fight. They march in numbers that have not been seen since the time of the Horus Heresy, for they recognise this time for what it is: the last, great war that will either see the Imperium cast down in ruin or standing triumphant over the bodies of traitors and xenos alike. To this decisive conflict they give their all, for honour demands no less.

A LEGACY OF HONOUR

The origins of the Knight worlds lie far back in Mankind's forgotten past, before even the rise of the Emperor on Terra. These bastions of Humanity have endured for millennia, fortified against the encroaching darkness, accumulating material resources and preserving ancient technologies.

It was during Mankind's first great exodus into the stars that the Knight worlds were established. Filled with hope and trepidation, swathes of human colonists struck out aboard the aptly named Long March ships that took decades to reach their pre-scouted destination worlds. These exoplanets were carefully chosen for their bounteous natural resources, as well as their theoretically habitable biospheres. The brave colonists – who had left behind everything they ever knew for a chance at extending human dominion across the galaxy – were quick to discover that habitable did not always mean safe.

Some worlds were infested with lethal flora and fauna that did their best to devour the colonists whole. Others were wreathed in ferocious storms, or were already inhabited by indigenous species that resented the alien interlopers who had washed up on their shores. Even more were made inhospitable by dangerous environmental factors such as exotic radiation, volcanic activity or viral outbreaks.

The raw materials required by the colonists to create their founding settlements came from cannibalising the ships themselves. As such, they had no way to flee their dangerous new homes, and no choice but to dig in and prevail. Some colonies, of course, were lost. Yet a far greater percentage successfully took root. This was thanks to a combination of the indomitable human spirit and the miracle that was Standard Template Construct technology.

STC machines could each replicate, endlessly and faultlessly, a specific device. They created atmospheric shelters, tools for farming and construction, means of power, transportation and the like. They also created the towering bipedal constructs known as Knight suits. These armour-plated walkers could traverse even the most perilous landscapes, endure the worst conditions that the colony worlds could throw at them, and – when suitably armed – fight in defence of the colonists themselves.

Few xenos races had an answer to these mechanical giants. Manufactured in large numbers, piloted by the most skilled and charismatic of the colonists, the Knights served as the mailed fist of human colonial expansionism. They smashed threats to Mankind's new domains wherever they encountered them, and their pilots rapidly achieved a status somewhere between celebrity and war hero. What no one realised was that even as the Knight suits were serving the colonists, their Thrones Mechanicum were irreversibly altering the minds and souls of those who piloted them.

Whether this was an intentional facet of the Knight STC, or some strange ghost in the machine, is ultimately irrelevant. The fact was that the longer the Knights

The Knights of House Terryn storm into battle, guns blazing and ion shields flaring with protective energies as their foes pour desperate fire into their immense attackers. The enemy's efforts will come to naught, for when the iron heel of Terryn descends, the Emperor's enemies are ground to blood and dust.

fought for their settlements, the more authoritarian their pilots became. Within a few generations, the concepts of chivalric conduct, ritual observance, loyalty and fealty that the Thrones Mechanicum implanted had indelibly changed the cultural dynamic of the human colonies. The Knight pilots became the first Nobles, and formed the original knightly houses. Those they protected took on an increasingly servile role, soon adopting the station of a feudal labour class.

The Knight worlds became ever more conservative and insular. They rejected advances in human technology and were slowly sidelined. They became a source of amusement to the intellectually and culturally superior masses of Humanity. Ironically, it was the Knight worlds' very isolationist nature and refusal to adopt new technologies that would protect them from the horrific apocalypse that devastated the rest of Mankind.

ALONE IN THE DARK

Humanity's fall was swift and terrible. Emergent psykers drowned worlds in warp storms and daemonic incursions. Thinking machines carried out genocidal purges. Gene-wars buried entire star systems beneath writhing tides of fleshy abominations.

The Knight worlds had burned their psykers as witches. They had turned away the thinking machines, citing the value of hard labour and a distrust of artificial intelligence. They had left their genetics untouched. Now, they stoked their watchfires, bolstered their defences and simply endured.

Thousands of years passed. The darkness of Old Night persisted, yet so too did the Knights and their people. Cultures regressed and technologies wore down, yet amazingly few Knight worlds succumbed to the dangers of a hostile galaxy. They maintained their traditions, fought to defend their borders, and waited for dawn to come.

The light of that dawn was the Emperor, and its spreading rays were the fleets of the Great Crusade. It was a Rogue Trader by the name of Jeffers who first rediscovered a Knight world, and in his reports to the Administratum, he advocated the potential usefulness of both the planet's Noble defenders and its raw material wealth.

More envoys followed in Jeffers' footsteps, and within decades, hundreds of Knight worlds had been brought into the Imperial fold. They soon proved their worth, their warriors marching into battle against the enemies of the nascent Imperium. Alien worlds shook beneath their tread. Enemies uncounted fled their terrifying might.

When the disastrous Horus Heresy embroiled the Emperor's realm in civil war, some of those Knight worlds turned traitor alongside their off-world masters. Yet many more – shielded from spiritual corruption by the conditioning of their Thrones – put down any rebellious elements within their own societies before joining the battle on the side of the loyalist Space Marine Legions. They proved their honour on untold bloody battlefields, and continued to do so in the ten millennia that followed. To this day, the surviving Knight worlds are vital lynchpins of the Imperial defence in countless sectors, protecting their allies from xenos and heretic invaders. All the while, their crusading armies take the fight to the Imperium's foes, crushing them wherever they are found.

THE OMNISSIAH'S BOON

The Adeptus Mechanicus rules over a swathe of planets scattered across the Imperium. Known as forge worlds, these are places of endless industry and rampant pollution, where the priests of the Omnissiah jealously hoard their secrets and lore. They are also military strongholds, whose strength is often augmented by alliances with knightly households.

FORGE WORLDS

Most knightly houses, though by no means all, are associated with a forge world, and in return for fighting alongside that forge world's Skitarii and Titan Legions, they gain access to advanced technology and knowledge that only the Adeptus Mechanicus possess.

The association between the knightly houses and the Adeptus Mechanicus dates back to the time of the Great Crusade. When the Knight worlds were first rediscovered, the different organisations that made up the Great Crusade competed ferociously with each other to gain control of the valuable resource the Knights represented. This Machiavellian political contest went on for decades, until the Mechanicum of Mars was finally able to establish their dominance in the fight to exploit the Knight worlds. The Mechanicum were driven in this by a desire to gain control of the archeotech that could be found in abundance on the ancient Knight worlds, but were also aware that the vast natural resources and military might of the knightly houses could make them a valuable asset. To this end, once they had established their right to exploit the Knight worlds, they set about making them dependent upon the Mechanicum for their continued survival.

At the time of the Great Crusade, the Tech-Priests' fleets found an anarchic galaxy where the ancient confederacy of interdependent human planets no longer existed. The surviving Knight worlds that were discovered had not retained all of their old technology, and had been forced to improvise comparatively crude repairs with the materials and techniques available. The Tech-Priests settled amongst these feudal empires, founding many forge worlds and establishing contacts within the knightly houses. They traded with the Knight worlds and investigated ancient ruins upon their surface, where relics of the Age of Technology could still sometimes be found. The Knights themselves proved invaluable in combating enemies such as marauding Orks. In return, the Tech-Priests promised technical expertise and helped the Nobles to rebuild their planets.

The most important thing that the Tech-Priests brought to the Knight worlds was the capability to maintain the Nobles' Knight suits. Over the course of the Age of Strife, much of the knowledge and many of the skills needed to keep the complex Knight armour working had been lost. Local technicians and artificers did their best to maintain the suits, but in many cases, they simply did not have the necessary ability. When the Knight worlds were rediscovered, most had only a handful of operational suits remaining, and even these were in a poor state. The Mechanicum promised to remedy this situation by inducting the local technicians that had been caring for the armour into the Cult Mechanicus, and teaching them how to keep the Knight suits in good repair. Because of this, nearly all suits of Knight armour bear the mark of the Cult Mechanicus as a reminder of the debt they owe to Mars.

Over the millennia, the forge worlds have grown powerful with the Knight worlds flourishing alongside them. Vast Mechanicus vessels regularly deliver new Knight suits, weapons, tools and mining machinery to the Noble houses, and leave with their holds packed with ores and food. In many places – especially beyond the Great Rift, in the Imperium Nihilus – the Tech-Priests and the Knights have become almost entirely dependant on each other. Many forge worlds form the hub of micro-empires, holding out against invading tides of xenos and heretics with the help of Noble households.

In exchange, the Knights have gained much from the Tech-Priests, their worlds gradually returning to being technically sophisticated cultures. However, the relationship between forge world and Knight world is not always an easy one. Even those knightly cultures that wholly adopted the worship of the Omnissiah, and whose Nobles swear fealty to the Fabricator General of Mars, are strong-willed warriors. Their codes of honour do not allow them to follow the commands of the Mechanicus without question, a fact that has frustrated many a cynical and duplicitous Martian priest.

Meanwhile, those worlds pledged to the rule of Terra and the worship of the Emperor can be more difficult still. Their Nobles are often mistrustful of the secretive Adeptus Mechanicus, and – beyond trading with them where they must – they typically keep the Tech-Priests at arm's length. The only exception to this is in the training of these worlds' Sacristans.

THE SACRISTAN ORDERS

The skilled artisans who maintain the Knight suits are known as Sacristans. Though their exact appearance, customs and organisation vary from one Knight world to the next, the Sacristans are typically monastic figures who maintain a certain distance from those outside their order. All are inducted into the holy mysteries of the Omnissiah within the tech-shrines of their closest forge world, and thus exhibit many of the same traits as the Tech-Priests themselves. Yet Sacristans are influenced also by the culture of the world they serve, a factor that affects their behaviour and appearance both. Thus, while the Sacristans of House Terryn wear fine data-robes of blue and red, and go about with their shaved heads held high, those of House Cadmus wear rubberised crimson cassocks and keep their faces covered at all times.

Depending upon the Knight world they serve, the Sacristan orders are viewed variously as wise savants, hidebound engineers, or even suspiciously secretive potential spies of the Adeptus Mechanicus. Whatever the case, the first duty of the Sacristans is to the Knights of their world, and it is one they discharge with tireless dedication and skill. It is the Sacristans who chant the devotional rites and apply the sacred unguents to appease each Knight suit's machine spirit. It is they who run repairs on each war engine, who calibrate its systems and see to it that the Knight's heraldry is always pristinely displayed. So dedicated are many Sacristan orders that they even follow the Knights to war, either doing their work between battles or else riding out in armoured crawlers, lumbering forge-landers or swift servitor-striders to perform repairs in the field.

SACRISTAN FORGESHRINES

The Sacristan orders deliver support to their Noble masters upon the field of battle. While some take to war zones in person aboard repair vehicles, many rely upon the forward deployment of various structures from which to operate. Perhaps the most common of these fortified support platforms is the Forgeshrine, an armoured refuelling depot whose servo-armatures can effect rapid repairs upon battle-damaged Knights. In the main, such structures are operated remotely by Sacristans behind the lines, though they also serve as forward workshops for sanctioned artificers such as Tech-Priest Enginseers or Techmarines.

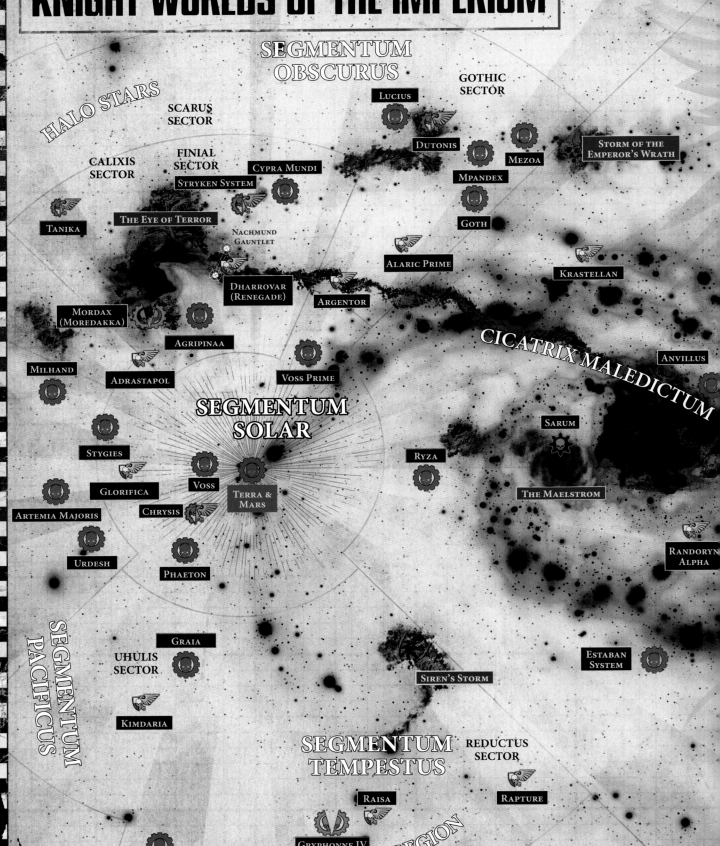

KNIGHT WORLDS OF THE IMPERIUM

SEGMENTUM OBSCURUS

HALO STARS

SCARUS SECTOR

GOTHIC SECTOR

Lucius

Dutonis

Mezoa

CALIXIS SECTOR

FINIAL SECTOR

Cypra Mundi

Mpandex

STORM OF THE EMPEROR'S WRATH

Stryken System

Tanika

The Eye of Terror

Goth

Nachmund Gauntlet

Alaric Prime

Krastellan

Dharrovar (Renegade)

Argentor

CICATRIX MALEDICTUM

Mordax (Moredakka)

Agripinaa

Anvillus

Milhand

Adrastapol

Voss Prime

Sarum

SEGMENTUM SOLAR

Ryza

Stygies

The Maelstrom

Glorifica

Voss

Terra & Mars

Artemia Majoris

Chrysis

Randoryn Alpha

Urdesh

Phaeton

SEGMENTUM PACIFICUS

Graia

Estaban System

UHULIS SECTOR

Siren's Storm

Kimdaria

SEGMENTUM TEMPESTUS

REDUCTUS SECTOR

Raisa

Rapture

Gryphonne IV

THE VEILED REGION

Zhao-Arkkad

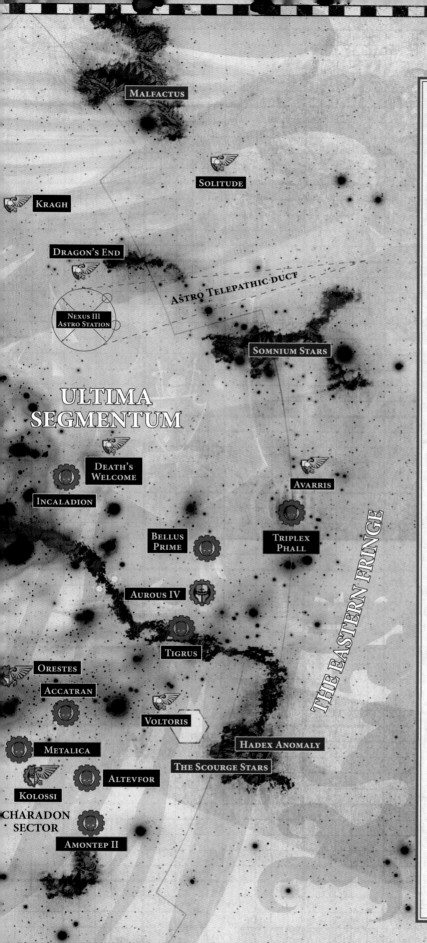

MALFACTUS

SOLITUDE

KRAGH

DRAGON'S END

ASTRO TELEPATHIC DUCT

NEXUS III
ASTRO STATION

SOMNIUM STARS

ULTIMA
SEGMENTUM

DEATH'S
WELCOME

AVARRIS

INCALADION

BELLUS
PRIME

TRIPLEX
PHALL

THE EASTERN FRINGE

AUROUS IV

TIGRUS

ORESTES

ACCATRAN

VOLTORIS

METALICA

HADEX ANOMALY

THE SCOURGE STARS

ALTEVFOR

KOLOSSI

CHARADON
SECTOR

AMONTEP II

Scattered across the black pall of space can be found many hundreds of Knight worlds. It has long been assumed by the lords of Terra and their administrators that the great majority of surviving Knight worlds have been returned to the fold of Mankind – they are either paying the Imperial tithe on those planets affiliated with the Imperium, or have allied themselves more closely with the Adeptus Mechanicus.

However, the galaxy is vast, and those bold early explorers travelled far and wide. There is much that still remains unexplored by the Imperium, and it is possible that there exist some far-flung Knight worlds that have not yet regained contact with Humanity.

Since the catastrophic manifestation of the Great Rift, many loyal Knight worlds have been cut off in the Imperium Nihilus. Dark forces besiege them from without, even as mutants and madmen rise up from within. Yet the Knight worlds have been here before, and their traditions and rituals are purposely designed to stave off the terrors from without. Brave and resolute, they are lighting their watchfires once more, even as they despatch crusading lances to aid their neighbouring worlds and systems. Not for twenty millennia have the Knights been so desperately needed as champions and protectors of Mankind.

KEY

 Questor Imperialis
Knight World

 Questor Mechanicus
Knight World

 Forge World

 Fallen Forge World

 Dark Mechanicum World

QUESTOR IMPERIALIS WORLDS

Imperial Knight worlds are typically ruled over by one or more Noble houses, each with their own heraldry, insignia, traditions and character. Though often hidebound and intractable on matters of honour, the Noble houses make for powerful allies, and when they send their Imperial Knights to war, the enemies of the Emperor tremble.

Questor Imperialis worlds vary enormously in appearance. Bleak, mountainous wastelands, hard-edged idylls of deep forests and rolling plains, airless deserts dotted with hab-domes, primordial wildernesses of volcano-studded jungle, ocean-locked island worlds and countless others all support knightly civilisations. Yet as much as each of these worlds differ, and as much as those differences have done to shape the societies that inhabit them, certain similarities hold true across virtually every Imperial Knight world in the Emperor's realm.

All Imperial Knight worlds are feudal, divided into fiefdoms or whatever other local term is given. Each of these territories is ruled over by one or more Nobles, its people labouring, farming, herding and producing in his or her name. In return, their knightly rulers offer them protection from whatever threats may descend from the stars. Each Knight in turn owes their allegiance to a high-ranking local leader, most commonly known as a Baron – though, again, local terms are myriad. Whether they be a marshal or a countess, a seneschal or a marchioness, each of these local rulers ultimately owes their allegiance to the High Monarch of their world. On some Knight worlds, each Baron may be the head of a separate Noble house. On others, a single Noble house holds sway across the entire planet. These mighty martial entities are known as the Great Houses, and include such ancient institutions as Terryn, Griffith, Hawkshroud and Cadmus.

The cultures of these worlds can vary hugely, from repressive patriarchies or matriarchies to martial meritocracies in which any Noble can rise to command if their lance arm is strong enough. Most sustain large-scale farming and mining operations. Combined with relatively low population densities and a lack of heavy industry, this ensures that the Imperial Knight worlds have remained comparatively unspoilt despite millennia of human occupation. Of course, in such a dark and dangerous age, many have been scarred forever by the horrors of all-out war, and even the most apparently paradisical world may harbour mutation, sedition and madness – dangers that its rulers must watch for constantly.

The word of each world's High King or Queen is law. It is certainly true that Noble houses may engage in a degree of politicking, and in extreme cases may settle their disputes through knightly jousts or even border skirmishes. Yet when the world's ruler issues the call to war, it is a source of endless dishonour to refuse their summons. Setting aside all other responsibilities, the Nobles link themselves into their Thrones Mechanicum, awaken their mighty Knight suits and march out to join the endless war for the Imperium of Mankind.

In truth, it takes very little provocation for a Noble to mount their Throne. Not only is the heady rush of power an intoxicant in its own right, but it is also the antithetical remedy to the tedium of courtly life. The ancient traditions and rituals of the Noble houses might have done much to stave off the corruption of Old Night, but they have also become sprawling affairs, and the few hours not

> 'These Chaos traitors slink from the shadows like scavengers come to pick a carcass clean. They believe that their cause is already won, arrogant vermin that they are. It will be my great and personal pleasure to disabuse them of this notion. Gather the banners! Sound the clarion call! House Vostris marches to war!'
>
> - High Queen Terenicia Asmosali Vostris, before the Relief of Corphan's Reach

consumed by such observances are inevitably spent seeing to the needs of the serf classes or dealing with matters of state.

Thus the Imperial Knights take to the battlefield the first chance they get, departing in their towering steeds amidst much fanfare and celebration. Whether answering a call for aid from an Imperial commander on campaign, responding to the distress call of some neighbouring world, or setting off on a crusade to avenge a perceived slight against the tenets of the Code Chivalric, the Knights march out in formations known as lances. Often their armies will consist of a handful of such formations led by a sufficiently powerful Baron.

When the peril is truly great, the High Monarch will lead the march in person. At such times, they stride to war at the head of their Exalted Court, a gathering of the highest ranking of the planet's Knights. Sometimes these are the closest of the ruler's personal household: cousins, siblings, uncles and the like. Other Exalted Courts are made up of the world's lesser rulers, who set aside their own seniority for a time to fight at the side of their liege. Whatever the case, these exceptional Knights are terrifying to behold on the field of battle, their mastery as warriors and commanders second to none. When the Exalted Court leads a planet's knightly lances to war, Imperial victory almost inevitably follows.

QUESTOR MECHANICUS WORLDS

Through mutual oaths and unbreakable vows, the Adeptus Mechanicus have forged alliances with many Knight worlds. In return for technical aid and reciprocal protection, these Questor Mechanicus houses send forth their adamantine Knight suits to honour any request made by their allies.

Those knightly houses closely aligned to the Adeptus Mechanicus are regularly called upon by the Martian Priesthood to uphold their ancient pacts. Most often, the Tech-Priests request military contingents from Knight worlds to accompany the Titan Legions into battle. The chosen Nobles are tasked with fighting directly in support of the legion's larger Battle Titans, or are asked to operate independently as scouts to protect the flanks of the slower-moving war machines. The Adeptus Mechanicus also petitions for Knights to join Explorator fleets, for they add invaluable firepower to contingents sent out to seize lost archeotech. When a threat is deemed sufficient, Knights are also asked to help defend key planets – especially endangered forge or mineral worlds. In return for such military aid, the Knight worlds receive greater technological resources.

To honour the more routine requests, a Noble house might send a single Knight, one of the honoured Barons and an escort of his knightly vassals, or perhaps a lance made up of Knights selected for the task in question. Occasionally, the Adeptus Mechanicus will decree that such seconded detachments must remain with a Titan Legion permanently; in these cases, the Nobles change their vows of allegiance and heraldry to reflect the legion they now serve.

HONOUR THE OMNISSIAH

While those Knight worlds sworn directly to Mars share many of the feudal structures and traditions of Questor Imperialis worlds, there can be no doubt that they possess less martial and cultural autonomy than their Imperial-aligned counterparts. Conclaves of tech-magi are a regular sight upon these planets, envoys from local forge worlds that walk the corridors of the knightly houses and maintain a silent, watchful presence during their rituals. The Nobles of such Knight worlds are, themselves, more tightly bound into the worship of the Omnissiah, often exhibiting the cog of the Adeptus Mechanicus, electoo designs carved into their flesh, robes coloured in the hues of their patron forge world, and mechanical augmetics that help them mesh more closely with the systems of their Knight suits.

The Knight worlds themselves also bear the inevitable scars that the touch of the Adeptus Mechanicus leaves. Vast strip-mines, churning manufactora and continent-sized agriplexes are common facilities that allow the Mechanicus to more efficiently exploit the planets' resources.

For all this, the Nobles of such a world are no less proud, honourable or strong-willed. They still rule their domains, march out to protect their borders, and owe ultimate fealty to their world's supreme ruler, who most often takes the title of Princeps. The appearance of Questor Mechanicus Nobles is generally more sombre than that of their counterparts in the Imperial-aligned Knight houses, and they are often less unruly and headstrong. Their ties to the Sacristan orders are strong, untroubled by suspicions of divided loyalties. Their battle doctrines are bellicose and expertly cogitated, while the bond that each Noble forges with their Throne Mechanicum and the machine spirit of their Knight suit is nigh symbiotic. When the lances of the Questor Mechanicus Knights go to battle, they do so with devastating efficiency and absolute, unified conviction.

The killing fields of Umekha burned. The Vostroyan 17th were in full retreat, snapping off shots as they fled across the veldt. Their persecutors followed, the android bodies of the Necrons reflecting firelight as they loosed volleys of shots into the fleeing Imperial Guard.

Baron Griegor of Taranis watched the spectacle through the auspicators of his Knight Warden, Iron God. He was still distant from the fight, but every ground-pounding stride brought him closer. The strategic situation scrolled across his retinas, projected from his data-manifold. Griegor's lip curled in distaste. It was not optimal.

'They are as honourless as they are merciless, these Necrons,' he said. 'It will be a pleasure to exterminate them.' Iron God's machine spirit rumbled its agreement.

'I concur, my liege,' voxed Lady Melandra of Taranis. Her Knight Gallant, Retributor, marched some twenty yards to his right, pennants fluttering in the hot winds of war. 'It is time to strike.'

'Agreed,' said Griegor, drinking in targeting data, atmospheric analyses and strategic auguries through the neural jacks in the base of his skull. 'We are within Code-stipulated combat range. Engage at will, my lady.'

Melandra's Gallant increased its stride, accelerating to a ponderous lope. Baron Griegor selected his targets with retinal twitches, flesh-hands and mechadendrites flying over his control console as he primed the spirits of his weapons and commanded them to let fly.

His avenger gatling cannon span up to speed, its scream carrying across the plain as it spewed fire into the advancing Necrons. Metal bodies detonated and came apart as thousands of foot-long shells tore through them. Rockets leapt away from his carapace launcher, adding billowing explosions to the mayhem. The Necron advance slowed, the surviving androids turning in eerie lockstep and swinging their guns to bear.

Griegor's ion shield flared blue as a hail of shots struck it, splashing harmlessly from its energised barrier. Then Retributor hit the Necron line, crushing warriors underfoot and hurling their hovering war engines through the air with every swing of blade and fist. While the Necrons' formation collapsed, Griegor fed power to his motive actuators and advanced to join the fray. As he did, his audio receptors transmitted a new sound that brought a thin smile to his lips. The Imperial Guard were cheering.

KNIGHTS AT WAR

When armies of Imperial Knights take to the battlefield, they employ the time-honoured strategies and tactics that have brought them victory for thousands upon thousands of years. High impact, dynamic and utterly destructive, their approach to war is as stirring a spectacle for their allies as it is terrifying for their enemies.

Whether they be Questor Imperialis or Questor Mechanicus, when the knightly houses go to war they adhere strictly to the tenets of the Code Chivalric and the martial structures of their worlds. Though their ways may seem archaic or convoluted to outsiders, the Knights' implicit understanding of the rules by which they fight, coupled with the whispered guidance of the ghosts in their Thrones, ensure an efficiency impossible to match by more sprawling Imperial armies.

At the head of every knightly host marches its most senior Noble. Whether this be the High Monarch or Princeps, a member of their Exalted Court, or a Baron of lesser standing, this individual's word is law. It is a rare Noble who would risk the dishonour of refusing a direct order from their liege. Below the force's commander, the remaining Nobles know their own place within the strata of the army, but all respect their comrades' right as Nobles to follow their instincts and fight where and how they see fit. Providing they obey the Code and their liege, Knights are permitted to fight more like a band of crusading heroes than an army of rank-and-file soldiers.

Knight suits can be categorised into different classes, each of which is constructed to a different STC pattern. By far the most common class of Knight is the Questoris, a tall and versatile chassis characterised by its comprehensive data-manifold, potent machine spirit and versatile armament mounts – one at each arm coupling, and an optional third atop its carapace. Questoris-class Knights can be further categorised by their traditional armaments into Errant, Paladin, Warden, Gallant, Crusader, Preceptor and various other patterns, each of which has its own strategic strengths.

To form the core of their battle lines, the Noble houses call upon the hulking Dominus-class Knights. More bulky than those of the Questoris class, these indomitable war engines boast dual plasma cores that – while potentially volatile when badly damaged – allow them to mount an intimidating array of heavy weaponry spread across two brachial couplings and three carapace mounts. Though typically fielded in smaller numbers than the Questoris, Dominus Knights provide their comrades with potent fire support.

The lighter Armiger-class Knights, akin to squires or a hunter's beaters, are piloted by minor Nobles or elevated household guards. Instead of sitting the full Throne Mechanicum, Armiger pilots don the Helm Mechanicus, a device that allows them to control their Knight but also neurally bonds them to a higher-ranking Noble. For all their lesser status, however, every Bondsman is a valued member of their household, and every Armiger is still a towering engine of destruction. Armigers typically fight in packs of two or more, and are employed to scout ahead, perform swift flank-attacks, and drive the enemy from cover and into the guns of the larger Knights on the orders of their bond-liege.

Most Knight armies consist of a core of Questoris Knights deployed in formations of three to five known as lances, supported by walking batteries of Dominus Knights and preceded by fleet-footed packs of Armigers. Though some houses are famed for their specialist types of lance, or predispositions towards specific classes of Knight, these tactics have brought the Nobles victory for many thousands of years.

KNIGHT CLASSES

While the STCs for some classes of Knight have been lost over the millennia, several remain in widespread use. Thus, while the mainstay of most households is the Questoris-class Knight chassis, heavy fire support is offered by the hulking Dominus-class engines, while scouting and raiding duties often fall to the lighter Armiger-class Knights.

STRUCTURE OF A
QUESTOR IMPERIALIS GREAT HOUSE

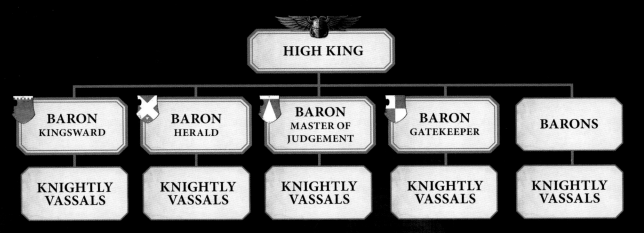

At the head of every Questor Imperialis Great House is a High King or Queen. Directly beneath the High Monarch in rank are their Barons, each a lord in their own right, owning some stronghold or key territory. All Barons owe allegiance to their High Monarch, but not all Barons are equal. Although each Knight world maintains their own rituals and hierarchy, the highest ranking Barons are those the High Monarch has selected to join their Exalted Court. These are the most loyal and veteran of their Nobles, and typically rule the largest swathes of territory.

Each Baron is responsible for their fiefdom – the lands that owe them tribute. Those Nobles beneath the Baron are their vassals; at their lord's call these Knights will assemble for war, and can also be called upon directly by their High Monarch or members of the Exalted Court.

The Knights themselves fight individually or in formations called lances. These are often made up of the vassal Knights of different Barons, constructed according to each member's individual talents, renown and determination.

STRUCTURE OF A
QUESTOR MECHANICUS GREAT HOUSE

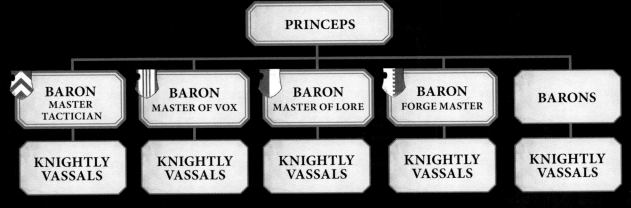

Knightly Great Houses aligned to the Adeptus Mechanicus are organised in a manner similar to their Imperialis cousins. The ruler of the Great House is known as a Princeps, and their decree is final. The rank below Princeps is that of Baron, and positions within this rank are still hierarchical, based on the individual Baron's influence and experience. For a Questor Mechanicus Great House's ruling council – also called an Exalted Court – the Princeps will promote four Barons. Known as Barons Prime, these individuals are second in power only to the Princeps themself.

Each Baron will have vassals beneath them, who are duty-bound to muster should they be called to battle. The exact number and organisation of these vassals varies wildly, depending upon the size and power of the knightly Great House in question. Regardless, when the summons to war is received, groups of oath-sworn Knights and entire detachments will be drawn from the Great House's strength. Only in unusual circumstances will the Princeps, or one acting in their stead, choose to select only from a single Baron's vassals.

QUESTOR IMPERIALIS HERALDRY

A Knight's rank is discerned by the stripes across their carapace armour. These stripes differ in colour for each house, but are always sympathetic to the house's normal livery.

High Monarch

Baron

Knight

Whatever a Knight's household, their tabard will always feature certain details. Their house's crest is borne in full, alongside the Knight's personal emblem and a number of his or her proudest battle honours.

HERALDIC PRINCIPLES

These elements of a Knight's panoply are the same for all members of their household.

These aspects of a Knight's heraldry are unique to each individual.

- ⬤ Full house crest
- ◯ House emblem
- ◼ House livery
- ◼ Imperial livery (typically red or black)

- ◉ Personal emblem
- ◼ Personal livery

HERALDRY IN PRACTICE

Sir Dunhand of House Hawkshroud, below, has livery typical of a Questor Imperialis Knight. Hawkshroud adopted black as a sign of their allegiance to the Imperium, and so bear this shade and the associated aquila on their suits' minor plates. Like many knightly houses, all members of this family have broadly similar personal heraldry – in this case, all include a laurel wreath. Hawkshroud is unusual in that these personal designs feature the insignia of forces they have allied with, and often campaign badges.

The honoured members of a house's Exalted Court each bear a specific design on their tilting plate, on top of which their house's icon is emblazoned.

Herald

Gatekeeper

Master of Justice

Kingsward

Battle honours, campaign markers and similar badges of prestige commemorate impressive kills as well as heroic actions performed upon the battlefield.

Order of the Executioner

Holy Ordos Alliance Icon

Legio Kill Marker

Munitorum Kill Honour

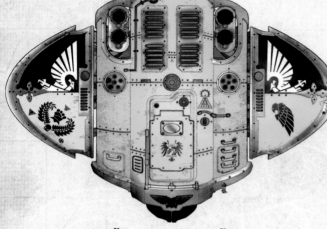

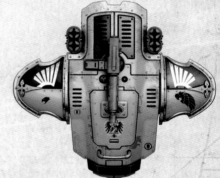

HOUSE TERRYN

No knightly house better exemplifies proud martial tradition than House Terryn. Its Nobles have fought unswervingly in the name of Humanity since the household was founded in the 25th Millennium. The house derives its name from Maximilian Terryn, first ruler of the tropical world of Voltoris, a planet colonised at the start of the Age of Strife. The practices and culture that Lord Terryn instituted are still honoured today. Indeed, each generation since has added to those ancient rituals, as they reaped their own battlefield triumphs worthy of remembrance. While much history has been lost over the long ages, the past glories of House Terryn have not been dimmed or been forgotten.

As for the Nobles themselves, the unending ceremonies honouring the house's storied past make them especially eager to go to war. When House Terryn forged their alliance with the Imperium, they ensured that Voltoris' law was changed so that any Knight under arms in the service of the Emperor was exempt from ceremonial obligations. Since that time, the Knights of House Terryn have sought out conflict across the galaxy, pursuing foes with an aggression born of years of unrequited yearning for war. Once a Terryn Noble has completed the Ritual of Becoming, they will join one of the Imperium's military campaigns, returning only rarely to their home world in order to show fealty and ensure the continuation of their line.

'Glory in Honour'

- *Motto of House Terryn*

THE EVOLUTION OF THE TERRYN CREST

In M25, Maximilian Terryn had visions of a mysterious white stallion that appeared to warn of danger. The horse's head on a blue field was taken as the emblem of his house.

In late M30, Lord Brutus Terryn led his house against the Great Kroktar, a beast that had plagued his people for a decade. When it was slain in the Battle of the Six Swords, details were added to the crest in honour of his victory.

It would be his descendent, Seuitonius Thucidides Terryn, who swore an oath of allegiance to the Emperor of Mankind, and amended his house's crest to honour their new status. Under his auspices, Terryn's Knights first fought alongside the Imperium's Ultramarines.

'YOUR CREST IS YOUR HONOUR. IT IS THE VISUAL EXPRESSION OF HEROIC DEEDS AND SELFLESS SACRIFICES BEYOND COUNT. IT IS THE SOUL OF YOUR HOUSE WORN PROUD FOR ALL TO SEE. PROTECT IT WHEREVER YOU CAN. SHIELD IT FROM THE FIRE AND FURY OF BATTLE AND SEE TO IT THAT, SHOULD THE CREST COME TO HARM, IT IS THE FIRST THING YOUR SACRISTANS RESTORE.'

- *Tenets of the Code Chivalric, 46th Vol*

MERCUTANE, ADAMANT WRATH

The stern Sir Mercutane is as unyielding as the gates of an armoured fortress. He is fortified in mind, body and soul by his unshakeable faith in the Emperor, and would gladly give his life in defence of the Imperium. Of course, Mercutane's enemies would not find that life easy to take, especially while he sits within the indomitable Knight Valiant known as Adamant Wrath. This Dominus-class war engine is infamously stubborn, its machine spirit refusing to yield no matter how much damage it suffers.

At Gallows Ridge, Adamant Wrath absorbed the fire of an entire renegade artillery company, weathering their punishing salvoes long enough to annihilate them with its own fearsome array of close-range armaments.

Such a pairing of resolute Noble and stalwart Knight has only served to magnify the strengths of both, and Adamant Wrath is currently known as House Terryn's most unshakeable defender.

TYBALT, FURY OF VOLTORIS

Tybalt is the High King of House Terryn, his esteemed rank denoted by the single cream band upon the carapace of his Knight Warden, the Fury of Voltoris. The crest of House Terryn is proudly displayed upon his tilting plate, and the white horse's head, the preeminent symbol of the house since its founding, is repeated often, including upon the gun shield of his avenger gatling gun. The Fury of Voltoris is further bedecked with battle honours and kill markings.

It is said that the full telling of High King Tybalt's triumphs takes well over twelve days to complete, and it is a tale that is still growing; the High King is ever eager to add whole new chapters to his ongoing saga of glory. In recent years Tybalt has taken up arms against the expansionist T'au Empire, first defending Voltoris from their invasion and later joining his forces to a wider Imperial crusade to drive the xenos back from the world of Agrellan and across the Damocles Gulf.

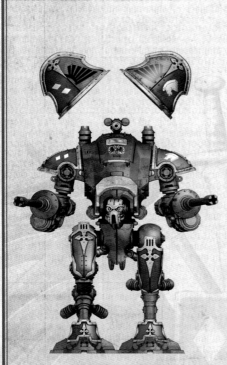

HESTER, CARNIVORE

Lady Hester is known for her rapier wit and keen aim. Her Helverin, Carnivore, responds swiftly to her commands.

TAURUS, HONOUR INTRACTABLE

The current Gatekeeper of House Terryn is Taurus, pilot of the Knight Errant known as Honour Intractable. To him falls the sacred honour of defending the strongholds of Voltoris, a duty that stretches back to the Old Night.

DARIUS, INTOLERANT

As Master of Justice, Baron Darius is the High King's chief military advisor and the appointed executioner of House Terryn's foes. He leads his own knightly vassals upon missions at Tybalt's command, bringing judgement in his lord's stead.

Though but a minor Noble, Sir Selwyn is a renowned duellist, using the chain-cleaver of his Warglaive to great effect.

BALTHAZAR, EVER-STALWART

To be Kingsward is both a great honour and tremendous burden, given not just to a superlative warrior, but to one whose loyalty is unquestionable. The clear choice for High King Tybalt was Baron Balthazar, pilot of the ancient Knight Ever-Stalwart. Members of Balthazar's direct bloodline have protected the rulers of House Terryn for seven generations; all have done their duty with distinction, honouring the quartered tilting plate that is the symbol of their office.

Ever-Stalwart is a legendary Knight Paladin. It is outfitted with the twin Icarus autocannon known as Skydoom, which has brought down aircraft, sail-finned Drakodons, and the winged broods of the Tyranids. In battle, Balthazar matches King Tybalt stride for stride, always angling his Knight and his ion shield to best protect his liege. It is also Baron Balthazar's task to guard Tybalt when the High King is not protected by his Knight suit, such as when he is holding court.

ALARBUS, HONOURED VIGILANCE

In his Knight Gallant, Honoured Vigilance, Sir Alarbus has already begun to forge a name for himself amongst his house's many heroes and veterans. To earn the blue and red stripes that honour both House Terryn and the Imperium, a Knight must single-handedly slay a Titan-class foe. Although still reckoned young, the Noble Alarbus has already done so twice, earning stripes for both his reaper chainsword and his thunderstrike gauntlet. He earned the first by felling a mountainous Gargant when his lance was sent to halt the rampages of Waaagh! Grazguts. Hard-pressed by the Gargant's guns, the intrepid Knight hacked through the Ork machine's protective plates before hoisting himself into the beast's iron belly, carving his way through and out the other side of the behemoth just before the Gargant's damaged engines exploded catastrophically.

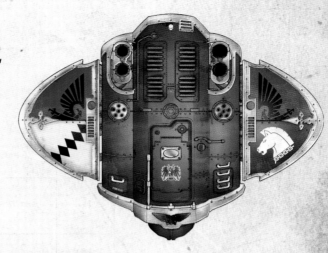

HOUSE CADMUS

Since first settling on the planet Raisa – located upon the very edge of the known galaxy – House Cadmus have taken great pride in their autonomous nature. For centuries only they protected the people of their world from the dark things that crawled, stalked and slithered through its arboreal forests. When the Imperium first made contact with the remote world they received a cold welcome from its Nobles, and it was many years before the first tentative alliances were formed. House Cadmus were equally resistant when forced to accept oaths with the forge world of Gryphonne IV, in return for skilled Sacristans and the technologies of the Adeptus Mechanicus.

Despite the enduring independence of its Nobles, House Cadmus has always honoured their allies' calls to arms. In recent times, when the shadow of Hive Fleet Leviathan fell over Gryphonne IV, the Knights of Raisa fought ferociously in its ultimately doomed defence. Although their fighting strength suffered greatly in the process, the destruction of the forge world freed House Cadmus from their obligations to the Tech-Priests, resulting in a change of allegiance that has been embraced by the current High King, Baron Roland of Swinford Hall.

The Knights of House Cadmus are peerless hunters. Indeed, the yearly Cull has been central to Raisan society for millennia, an event in which the Nobles compete to eradicate the verminous abhumans that infest their home world and, in doing so, hone skills that they put to use against the greater threats facing the Imperium.

'THEY WHO ARE NOT OUR ALLIES ARE OUR PREY'

- *Motto of House Cadmus*

WILLIAM, BLOODY BROADSWORD
Bold to the point of recklessness, Sir William is the latest Noble to pilot the Knight Paladin Bloody Broadsword.

MALCOLM, THE BEAST KILLER
Hero of the Battle of Thunderhead, Malcolm slew a bio-titan and was one of the few survivors of the fighting on Gryphonne IV.

ORLANDO, COWARD'S BANE

Orlando is next in line to become one of the Twelve Barons of Raisa, a position that would ordinarily mark out its occupier as a potential rival to the ruler of House Cadmus. However, Orlando's disregard for the annual Cull, an event of great significance on Raisa, ensures that he could never claim kingship of his house. For Orlando, slaying the beasts is an everyday task, not a sporting event. Thus, Orlando is content as ruler of Patton Hall, a keep in the most isolated province of Raisa.

When called to war, Orlando pilots Coward's Bane, his Knight Crusader. One of the eldest of Raisa's Knight suits, Coward's Bane still flashes emerald when its ancient ion shield repels a powerful incoming shot, a sure sign that its shield generators are truly ancient. Orlando's vassals all know well the thunderclap roar emitted when his Knight's gauntleted fist strikes home. It is a sound heard often enough, for Orlando is tasked with leading many campaigns – a tribute to his fighting prowess.

HOUSE GRIFFITH

The Knights of House Griffith are exemplary warriors who constantly strive to maintain the legacy of martial excellence established by their ancestors – the first colonists of Dragon's End, named for the winged drakes native to the world. As the legends go, before the STC Knight suits could be completed, the settlers were forced to fight the scaly beasts from horseback. The most accomplished of their number was Nathaniel Griffith, who slew three of the winged drakes with a dragonbone lance and eventually became the inaugural ruler of the newfound knightly house.

As part of their ancient traditions, the Nobles of House Griffith are raised on tales of daring valour and heroic deeds, and still ride horses and train with lance and blade. Disputes between Nobles are routinely settled with duels or jousts, while regular tournaments, such as the annual contest in the Field of Adamantium, see families compete for standing and prestige.

The result of these traditions is a knightly house of consummate bladesmen, each one seeking out the largest foes they can in battle and bringing them low with thundering charges and precise reaper blows. Indeed, the Knights of House Griffith crave such melee combat, and have earned a bloody reputation for aggressiveness in battle. In this way the spirit of the first dragon hunters lives on in the heart of every House Griffith Noble. Some rare surviving Thrones Mechanicum still hold memories from that time, filled with the ghostly whispers of long-dead heroes.

'HONOUR AND FURY, COURAGE AND STRENGTH'

- Motto of House Griffith

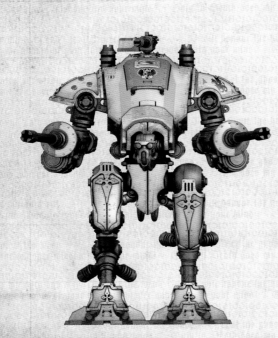

EDMANE, HOUND SINISTOR
An honoured Bondsman serving the famed Sir Tarthin, Edmane flushes his master's quarry from cover.

SARIS, HOUND DEXTRA
Bondsman Saris uses her Warglaive's firepower to scatter the foe in panic, the better for Sir Tarthin to hunt.

NATANYA, BANE OF IRON

Lady Natanya pilots the immense Knight Valiant known as Bane of Iron, whose machine spirit is amongst the most aggressive of all House Griffith's hunting steeds. Natanya herself is strong-willed and courageous, the only Noble ever to fully break the unruly Bane of Iron to their command. Natanya has harnessed her war engine's natural ferocity and destructive power, and now specialises in providing devastating close-range fire support to her comrades in the field.

Griffith's fine tradition of monster hunting has found a worthy proponent in Lady Natanya, who excels in obliterating the Daemon Engines of the Heretic Astartes. She was amongst the Knights seconded to Guilliman's Indomitus Crusade, and soon proved her valour by protecting her Ultramarines allies with her Knight's crackling ion shield while annihilating heretical war machines one after another with pinpoint fire. Natanya has shared an honour-bond with the sons of Ultramar ever since.

HOUSE HAWKSHROUD

There is no knightly house more loyal than House Hawkshroud. Its Nobles have cultivated an impeccable reputation for honouring their debts and keeping their word regardless of the personal cost, and those that enter into oaths of allegiance with Hawkshroud know that when they call for support it will be forthcoming. For this reason the Knights of Krastellan are often on campaign, fulfilling the promises of their lords and laying down their lives to uphold past alliances.

This culture of oath-debt is woven into the society of House Hawkshroud's home world of Krastellan, where even among the peasants a man's word is his bond. An eerie, haunted place, its desolate moors and black hills stretch in all directions under skies heavy with freezing rain. While other Knight worlds embrace a degree of technology, the Nobles of Krastellan see anything more than is required for the continued operation of their Knights as an extravagance and the first step on the road to weakness. So it is that much of Krastellan remains primitive, peasants farming the damp earth and herding cattle, while the Nobles live as their ancestors did ten thousand years before.

Unlike many other knightly houses, Hawkshroud's Knights often bear campaign markings, army badges and other such emblems demonstrating loyalty to those they have sworn to aid. These serve as a sign of dedication to the cause of their allies, and also act to strengthen the bonds of brotherhood between the Knights and those they fight alongside. After all, House Hawkshroud is proud to stand by those that have stood by them in the past.

'No Request For Aid Shall Be Denied'

- Motto of House Hawkshroud

MORLIAN, OATHKEEPER
Piloted by the sure-sighted Sir Morlian, Oathkeeper has slain fourteen enemy aircraft to date.

RITTER, HEADSMAN
The deposed Duke Ritter vents his anger and resentment by beheading the war engines and monsters of the enemy.

GARROCK, FORSWORN WRATH

Garrock serves as knightly vassal to Baron Raptallious, and has proudly answered his liege's call to war many times. He is one of the Oathsworn, a warrior sub-culture unique to House Hawkshroud. These Nobles develop such strong bonds with the Imperial forces they fight alongside that they stay on campaign far beyond the length of service that was initially offered or requested of them. In doing so the Oathsworn are, in essence, walking the path of the Freeblade Knight. Unlike true Freeblades, however, these lone Hawkshroud Knights continue to proudly bear their house's livery, and eventually seek to return to Krastellan, where they will be welcomed with honour.

BARTHANNEL, THE REVERED FURY

Sir Barthannel is the living example of House Hawkshroud's motto. A well-voyaged Baron, he has honoured debts across the galaxy, and fought alongside Astra Militarum regiments raised from over one hundred different planets, and no fewer than twelve Chapters of Space Marines.

Barthannel's Knight Crusader is the Revered Fury. It bears regalia from only the most memorable of his many campaigns, most notably the Brotherhood Honours presented to him by the Great Wolf Logan Grimnar of the Space Wolves himself. Because of his dedication to his duty, it has been many decades since Sir Barthannel stepped foot upon his home world, Krastellan. Now, though, having received word of the peril facing his Noble house, Barthannel makes haste to return at last and lend his might to the battle.

HOUSE MORTAN

By the time the antecedents of House Mortan had arrived upon Kimdaria, the mysterious nebula known as the Black Pall that surrounded the planet had grown unexpectedly dense. Fell creatures, already accustomed to the world's dim light, roamed the ink-black landscapes, and it was only through the skill and dedication of the colonists' Knights that the beasts were driven back and the first settlements established. For millennia after the Great Crusade, the Black Pall lingered over Kimdaria and its star system – not until late M35 did the impenetrable shroud partially dissipate, letting in a few diffused rays of sunlight and allowing the long-lost planet to be rediscovered by Mankind.

What they found was a bleak and ritualistically ordered world, a place where soaring walls separated civilisation from the monster-haunted darkness that lay beyond. From heavy gates the black Knights of House Mortan would regularly emerge, their constant patrols keeping the encroaching predatory behemoths at bay. The towering war machines had become as accustomed to the endless night as the beasts they hunted, the darkness of their home world seeming to cling to them even when standing in the light, and so as to better fight their obscured enemies, the Knights of House Mortan placed a premium upon close combat. It is a tendency that holds to this day, with Mortan's grim and taciturn Nobles expecting all battles to eventually come down to murderous work with their roaring reaper chainswords and crackling thunderstrike gauntlets.

'IN WAR, SHOW NO MERCY'

- *Motto of House Mortan*

DIRKWALD, BLACK HEART
Sir Dirkwald recently completed his thousandth watch-patrol on Kimdaria, allowing the Noble to serve off-planet.

LUDWIG, WAR STRIDER
The sign of a long-serving House Mortan war hero is the banded weapon, denoting a dozen Titan-class kills.

GERROLT, PRIDE OF BLACKCRAG

In House Mortan, high-ranking Knights and their positions within the household are identified by the pattern of yellow bands upon their hull; the lone stripe upon Gerrolt's Knight proclaims him as the High King. Despite – or perhaps because of – his lofty station, Sir Gerrolt is dour, even by the standards of his house. Many claim the reason for this is the Throne Mechanicum Gerrolt bonded with centuries ago – tragedy haunts this ancient artefact the way fell beasts lurk within the dark forests of Kimdaria.

Whatever dark whispers might fill Sir Gerrolt's mind, they do not seem to hamper his ability to rule over Kimdaria's people and lead House Mortan's Knights in battle, nor diminish the vehemence with which he destroys the enemy. Blasting rockets into the distance, blazing away with his avenger gatling cannon and smiting foes with his thunderstrike gauntlet, Gerrolt steers the Pride of Blackcrag into the thick of the fighting, slaughtering all that fall under its shadow.

QUESTOR MECHANICUS HERALDRY

HERALDIC PRINCIPLES

Identical for all members of the house

- ⬤ Full house crest
- ◯ House emblem
- ▮ Major Adeptus Mechanicus livery (typically red, silver or white)
- ▮ Minor Adeptus Mechanicus livery (typically yellow or black)

Like Imperial-aligned knightly houses, the members of a Mechanicus-aligned Exalted Court bear a specific design on their carapace to signify rank.

Princeps

Baron

Knight

Skitarii Alliance Icon

Duelling Medal

Blessed Laurel-cog

Badges and symbols, normally displayed upon the tabard, acknowledge the wearer's battle honours and celebrate their role in famous campaigns or alliances.

HERALDRY IN PRACTICE

The suit belonging to Sir Xantek of House Taranis, below, serves as an example of a Questor Mechanicus Knight. Although houses dedicated to the Machine God are less predisposed to tolerate personal heraldry, this does not, however, preclude individual differences. Here, Sir Xantek has chosen to paint the back half of his Knight's main carapace black, to signify that he marches always out of the shadow of ignorance and into the Omnissiah's light. Also of note is the common black-and-white half-toning of the Knight's faceplate.

A house's Barons Prime each sport a specific design on their tilting plate commensurate with their rank, displayed behind their house's icon.

Master of Vox   Forge Master   Master of Lore   Master Tactician

Questor Mechanicus houses follow several conventions in the markings on their banners; usually, these designs are black and white, and display the cog symbol of their allies above their battle honours.

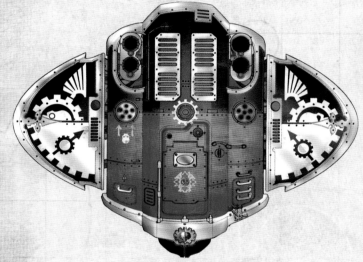

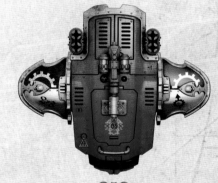

HOUSE RAVEN

Only a handful of cities remain on the Questor Mechanicus world of Kolossi, islands of steel and smoke amid the deep-core shafts and strip-mine canyons. Greatest of these is the Keep Inviolate, an immense stronghold whose glittering peak welcomes home the Nobles of House Raven as they descend from orbit into the planet's rolling banks of smog. The work of millennia, the Keep Inviolate is a fortress to rival the Fang on Fenris or the Emperor's Palace on Terra, its walls hundreds of feet thick and its macro cannon capable of tearing even the largest of spacecraft apart. The real power of the keep, though, lies in its Vault Transcendent. Dug into the bedrock, its heavily shielded halls house hundreds of Knight suits, each ready to stride out to battle as an unbreachable crimson wall.

The quantity of Knights House Raven can field is unmatched by any other household. Moreover, thanks to ongoing ambassadorial efforts, dozens of other households owe fealty to House Raven, swelling their might still further. While the armies of most knightly houses shake the ground with their stride, when House Raven deploys in force, their relentless, grinding advance creates a rolling thunder that unnerves even the most resolute foes.

House Raven maintains its power only through the strength of its alliance with the forge world of Metalica, a union that dates back to the time of the Great Crusade. Lord Gregor, Raven's then ruler, struck a deal with Metalica's Tech Adepts to ensure that his house had sufficient Sacristans to service his full host of Knights; these specialists became known as the Iron Brotherhood. In return, Gregor swore House Raven's eternal fealty to Metalica – a pledge his descendants have upheld to this day.

'Honour Inviolate, Kolossi Eternal'

- *Motto of House Raven*

THE EVOLUTION OF THE RAVEN CREST

In M24, Alistar Raven laid the ambitious foundations of the Keep Inviolate. So large did it loom in the minds of the house's Nobles that it would form the basis of their heraldry. For millennia after, each new ruler of House Raven added to this massive adamantium-plated edifice, and it now stands amongst the greatest strongholds of the Imperium.

In M28, Lord Grunwald formed the honourable Order of Companions. Its first leader was Lady Syrtana Raven, who saved Grunwald's life during the Kortasa Blitz. Shortly after, the crossed blades symbol of the order was incorporated into House Raven's crest. To this day, the most meritorious of Raven's Nobles endure the Trial of the Companions to join the order.

Three millennia later, Lord Gregor met the first emissaries from Metalica and swore enduring oaths of alliance with the Mechanicum. In exchange for skilled Sacristans, the Knights of House Raven would fight beside the Legio Metalica. Raven's crest was modified in respect of those oaths, and the house's strength grew under the forge world's patronage.

OMNITROS, PRIDE OF KOLOSSI

More than any other knightly house, Raven are able to use sledgehammer tactics and weight of numbers to crush their enemies underfoot. Sir Omnitros has become adept at supporting these tactics, constantly absorbing battlefield data and cogitating the optimal strategic solution with up-to-the-minute accuracy.

His Knight Castellan, Pride of Kolossi, has been augmented with additional auspicator arrays and data-looms to aid Omnitros'

efforts. With such a wealth of auto-analysed information flowing through his mind, Sir Omnitros lays down pinpoint volleys to support his comrades' advance, and projects his ion shields to cover them as they retreat. Whether attacking or defending, Pride of Kolossi operates as a lynchpin for the House Raven battle line, utilising predictive fire-patterns to blast each emergent threat as it appears and paving the way for overwhelming victory in the name of the Omnissiah.

DAKLORN, TEMPERED FURY

Baron Daklorn serves as Forge Master in the Exalted Court of Princeps Grevan. The only external sign of this honour is the crenelated marking upon the tilting plate of Tempered Fury. To the Forge Master falls the defence of the Keep Inviolate, ensuring that the immense fortress, long a symbol of House Raven's dominance, can repel even the most aggressive of assaults. Amongst his duties are the protection of entire armies of Sacristans and the mustering of the household Knights should the Iron Duke of Kolossi call.

Only those Barons with demonstrated loyalty and the highest battlefield honours are asked to join the Exalted Court, and Daklorn has proven himself in both regards many times over. His Knight Crusader, Tempered Fury, is a walking arsenal, allowing the Forge Master to lay down withering firepower with unerring accuracy. When not fighting as part of his Princeps' Exalted Court, Daklorn leads the Gateguard of the Keep Inviolate. Of late, he has faced – and crushed – numerous heretical armies.

WALKORN,
UNYIELDING IRON

Walkorn and his Knight, Unyielding Iron, have been inducted into House Raven's revered Order of Companions, chiefly for their actions against the Ork worlds of the Heloeum Drift. During the Battle for the Wilted Bastion, Walkorn personally destroyed the Rok *Eye of Mork*. Like all the Companions, Unyielding Iron bears no mark to distinguish its elite status, for House Raven holds that such iconography only benefits their enemies.

Despite this, Raven are proud adherents of the chevron designs that mark many Knights. Originally chevrons were used to mark the age of a Knight suit: those with the largest and widest marks were ancient pieces of archeotech. In time, the chevrons took on another meaning for House Raven, identifying the age and experience of its Nobles.

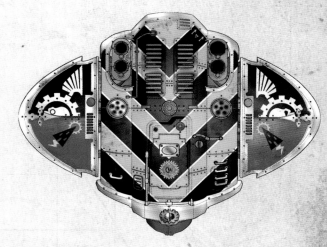

GREVAN, FERROUS MAXIMUS

Lord Grevan Raven, fourth of his name, is the Princeps of House Raven, the Iron Duke of Kolossi and he who sits upon the Adamantium Throne of the Keep Inviolate. A single white stripe on his Knight suit, Ferrous Maximus, denotes him as Princeps. As a young pilot he joined the Order of Companions – the fighting elite of the house – where all noted his martial prowess. His meteoric rise continued to the highest level, as befitted his Noble ancestry.

Though House Raven have access to many Knight suits, the majority of them are Errant and Paladin patterns. Ferrous Maximus, however, is a Knight Warden. As the legend goes, its avenger gatling cannon was thrice blessed by the Omnissiah himself. Whenever the Knight's need is greatest, the pilot of Ferrous Maximus can recall that ancient stored memory, spitting a rapid burst of impossibly accurate gatling cannon fire that shreds even the largest foe.

RANDUL, IMPENETRABLE

Randul is one of the many Barons that serve beneath Princeps Grevan. His peers claim he is cursed, for each engagement ends with his Knight catastrophically damaged. Yet each battle also ends in victory, usually thanks to Randul's heroics.

KARSTIN, HAMMERBLOW

Sir Karstin is a minor Noble who submits willingly to the mental dominance of Sir Krewald in return for greater standing.

KREWALD, GLORY UNBLEMISHED

Krewald and his Knight, Glory Unblemished, served with distinction alongside Legio Metalica's Titanicus, fighting in support of the Emperor-class Titan *Hand of Judgement* while it annihilated a turncoat city.

TOLOS, TRIUMPHAL

Sir Tolos is a more grudging Bondsman of Sir Krewald, but his recently diminished status allows for no other option.

HOUSE VULKER

Despite being one of the greater houses amongst those aligned to the Adeptus Mechanicus, House Vulker is reclusive and mysterious. Their home world is Aurous IV, a mineral-rich planet nestled in a crowded star system. It was to exploit the planets of this system, and surrounding asteroid belts, that the forge world Bellus Prime was established nearby. The bonds between Aurous IV and Bellus Prime remain tight, with the same golden-plated servitor creatures working upon both worlds.

The courts of House Vulker are singular places, full of Tech-Priests and servitors that speak in coded machine language and number sequences. They enact mechanical ceremonies that are, for the uninitiated, disturbing to look upon, their meanings unclear and vaguely sinister. The Nobles of House Vulker hide every inch of their flesh with robes, sometimes even wearing masks of gold. Outsiders are not welcome within their steel-clad fortresses.

When called to war, the Knights of House Vulker leave behind their curious trappings, striding out to do battle with all the surety of their peers. They place a premium upon well-coordinated plans for both attack and defence, always engaging the enemy at the optimal distance by utilising carefully cogitated trajectories. This often results in Vulker's Knights waiting patiently for the enemy to draw close before annihilating them with searing barrages.

'For the Gilded Glory of the Omnissiah'

- Motto of House Vulker

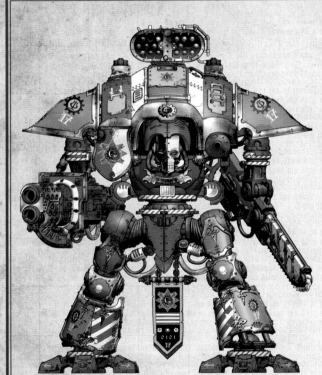

BARON GOLPHYTES, STRIDENT

Marked by his halved tilting plate, Golphytes is the Master of Lore, the keeper of sacred data, the Cogitator Prime.

KNIGHTLY TITLES

A consistent frustration experienced by the Administratum is the elaborate, often archaic forms of address used by the Noble houses. Not only does every Knight world have its own conventions, but even within the households of a single planet there may be multiple prefixes, suffixes and derivations that date back thousands of years.

Complicating matters further, in many knightly cultures it is considered deeply offensive to address a Noble incorrectly. Duels to the death have been demanded for less, and more than one officious Administratum clerk has had to be hustled from a Noble's presence in a flustered panic before they dig themselves any deeper into trouble. Imperial authorities persist in their attempts to learn these archaic systems of name and title, however, as they are a vital part of communicating with the Knights in battle.

Beyond the relatively straightforward titles of the High Monarch and their Exalted Court, the vast majority of Knight worlds tend towards sir or lady as a standard honour-prefix, although variations such as sire, sor and sirrah are not uncommon. Other worlds attach terms such as 'most honoured' or 'Become' after the Noble's name, or else a derivation of their home world such as 'ap Kostonor' or 'fon Medusar'. Multiple terms denoting standing within a world's knightly houses are not uncommon: a Knight of a ruling household might be Lady Eleanora Uhl Tassos, while a lesser Noble of the same world might be Sir Geralt Lor Tassos. There are as many of these complex honorifics as there are stars in Imperial skies, and all are of grave import to the Nobles who use them.

BARON VROTH, GILDED CONQUEROR

The twin stripes upon his Knight's carapace mark Vroth as a Baron, and the pattern upon his tilting plate denotes his position within the Exalted Court as Master of Vox. The Master of Vox, sometimes known as a Broadhailer, bears the internal comms equipment that can network together all the fighting detachments of House Vulker's Knights as well as broadcast vox hails to distant allies. In many Exalted Courts, the Master of Vox commands a rearguard position, focusing upon communications and lending supporting fire. Not so for Baron Vroth. In typical Knight Gallant fashion, Baron Vroth wades into the thickest of the fighting, crushing all before him. His Knight, the Gilded Conqueror, is one of House Vulker's eldest and most richly decorated suits. Only the most ancient of machines bear gilded armour burnished to a sheen, and the Gilded Conqueror boasts a full helm-plate made of precious metal.

LUXIOUS, UNALLOYED VICTORY

The display of bare adamantium armour plates is considered a deeply significant tribute by House Vulker. Lady Luxious earned this honour during fierce fighting on the death world of Tasmadar II, after Tyranid bio-horrors ambushed Baron Dyrok's lance. Surging from the overgrown slopes of the valley known simply as the Gullet, a pair of huge serpentine beasts crippled the Baron's Knight and toppled Sir Ulrecht's Gallant with a punishing body-blow. With icy calm, Luxious cogitated firing solutions and unleashed a punishing salvo of rockets and gatling fire that ripped one beast apart before it could finish Ulrecht's toppled steed. Unalloyed Victory went blade-to-chitinous-claw with the other Tyranid monster, sustaining heavy damage before finally bisecting the creature's head with its roaring chainsword. The Lady and her Knight stood guard over their damaged comrades for a further eight hours, seeing off predatory waves of bio-beasts before relief finally reached the Gullet. For this magnificent deed of valour, both Luxious and her steed were greatly honoured, their systems and panoply restored to full magnificence before the final push to liberate Tasmadar II.

HOUSE TARANIS

True servants of the Machine God, the warriors of House Taranis bear the honour of belonging to the first of the knightly houses, and although they bear the names of Noble and Knight, they do not follow the feudal ways of their kin.

Founded on Mars, where the original Knight suit was created in the Age of Technology, House Taranis have never been forced to survive on a frontier world or build keeps against the dark void, and so remain more akin to the Legio Titanicus than their peers from the Knight worlds. Equally, they are not in thrall to the Thrones Mechanicum like other Nobles, the subliminal neural conditioning that creates the rigid traditions of the Knights absent from their own Thrones. The Nobles of Taranis do not share the technological secrets behind this difference, seeing their own lack of conditioning as another hallmark of the Imperium's preeminent Knights.

The civil war that erupted on Mars during the Horus Heresy saw House Taranis suffer near total losses. As the internecine conflict drew to a close, just two Knights remained. Only incredible commitment, and the skill of Mars' Tech-Priests, saw House Taranis survive its darkest hour, and rebuild to be stronger than ever before. This experience has stayed with the Knights of House Taranis; they believe the Omnissiah will always protect them, no matter how dark the hour, and it is this faith that has so emboldened them since the Great Rift yawned wide.

'HONOUR THY FORGE, HONOUR THE PRIMUS ORDINUS'

- Motto of House Taranis

THASSOR, RED JACKAL

Sir Thassor considers himself an exterminator of unclean engines. His Armiger Warglaive, Red Jackal, has a predatory machine spirit, and together the two of them run down and execute traitor tanks without mercy.

XANTEK, BLADE OF MARS

Terribly wounded by a Chaos Titan, Xantek is one of the few Nobles who have survived the Ritual of Becoming twice. He believes himself the embodiment of his house's ability to rise again from darkness, and his faith is fervent indeed.

ARCHIMAXES, DEVASTATION UNBRIDLED

Sir Archimaxes rules over Hydraulach Point. This armoured keep overlooks the southern reaches of the Mare Erythraeum on Mars, and is intended as a shield against the predatory battle-servitors that periodically range out of their hunting grounds to threaten the manufactorums beyond. Archimaxes stands his vigil alone, and is happy to do so, for he is a solitary being who prefers the company of machines to that of living creatures. Archimaxes is only truly content when enthroned within his mighty Knight Castellan,

Devastation Unbridled, hunting down and eliminating corrupted servitor-monsters the size of dropships.

When he is called to war by the Princeps of House Taranis, Archimaxes speaks little to his comrades. Yet they are ever grateful for his taciturn presence, for he is diligent in his efforts to shield them from harm, and merciless in his persecution of the enemy's largest and most monstrous beasts.

HOUSE KRAST

Ten thousand years have not been enough to heal the bitterness that pervades House Krast. From atop shielded strongholds, its Nobles look with cold fury upon the toxic remains of their home world of Chrysis, knowing to whom they owe the blood-price for its death. Where once existed continents thick with plants and oceans teeming with life, now only skeletal, petrified forests and vast open basins remain. On shorelines turned from wave-washed beaches into dry towering cliff faces, and on islands rising up above empty seas, the crumbling ruins of long-dead knightly houses serve as a constant reminder of treachery.

Chrysis was the first Knight world to be rediscovered during the Great Crusade. Its Nobles showed no hesitation in joining the Emperor, making House Krast amongst the longest-serving defenders of Mankind's realm – a fact of which they remain rightfully proud. The treachery of the Horus Heresy took a fearsome toll on Chrysis, with the traitor Titans of Legio Mortis the chief culprits behind the utter ruination of the world. Krast was the only one of the world's knightly houses to survive the calamitous events, although so great were their losses that only the support of Mars allowed them to recover.

At that time, the surviving Nobles of House Krast swore two oaths: the first, eternal loyalty to the Red Planet; the second, eternal vengeance against those that betrayed them. Their descendants maintain these oaths to this day, honouring Mars while seeking out the forces of Chaos above all others.

'CRUSH THE SERPENT'

- Motto of House Krast

NARSUS, HATE'S REQUIEM

The machine spirit of the Armiger Helverin Hate's Requiem fights with a particular venom against traitors and turncoats, a trait its pilot, Bondsman Narsus, is more than ready to exploit.

KARYX, SERPENT'S BANE

Countess Karyx slew the Alpha Legion Chaos Lord Stentyrius, ending his machinations in a blast of superheated energies from the thermal spear of her Armiger Warglaive, Serpent's Bane.

LAGOS, REDEMPTION OF ADAMANT

Baron Lagos is the pilot of the Knight Crusader known as the Redemption of Adamant. In House Krast, the rank of Baron is signified by the twin yellow stripes atop the carapace. Over long years of service, the Redemption of Adamant has weathered the worst battle damage the enemies of Mankind could inflict, yet always the Sacristans have repaired its adamantium armour; if anything, Lagos and the myriad memory-figments within his Throne Mechanicum come back stronger each time, eager to exact revenge.

As a Baron, Lagos' duties are to maintain his stronghold, to lead the Knights under his service, and to answer the call of the Princeps should he summon members of House Krast to war. Depending upon his liege's needs, Baron Lagos might send a household detachment of his Knights, go into battle himself, or lead his own favoured escort – a Baronial Court – into battle.

FORILLUS, HEADTAKER

Forillus was seconded to the Cockatrices Titan Legion, and now bears their colours as part of his livery. During the years of his service alongside the Cockatrices, Sir Forillus learned many strategies of mechanised war, including how to engage enemy war machines even larger and deadlier than his own, and how to evade their fury long enough to wear them down and destroy them. These lessons proved invaluable when Forillus found himself fighting alongside the Vostroyan 87th against the vast war effigies of Waaagh! Cogstompa, making him the bane of the greenskins' most powerful battle engines.

FREEBLADES

Some Knights forsake their houses to wander alone amongst the stars, or else are cast out as exiles to face the same fate. Such warriors are known as Freeblades, and must carve out their own path to glory. Many quickly meet their end upon a battlefield far from home and kin, their past deeds buried with them – yet some prove themselves worthy of legend.

There is no one reason a Knight might become a Freeblade. Nobles who dishonour themselves, committing some unforgivable mistake, may be cast out of their household, or else decide themselves that they cannot remain. Some Freeblades are forged by force of circumstance; perhaps they were left stranded far from home, and have fought so long across the stars that solitude is all they now know. In other cases, entire knightly houses are destroyed, leaving a forsaken Noble to fight on for vengeance alone.

So do lone Knights set off into the vast void of space. Some quest for a worthy cause to uphold, others search out a great wrong that they might set right. Rarely Freeblades will become reclusive, willing to fight only to protect their hermitage, while others may even be driven mad by their isolation or the circumstances of their exile, becoming murderous destroyers or silent avengers more akin to supernatural beings than the proud warriors they once were. Whatever the case, Freeblade Nobles become ever more bonded to their Knight, human and machine living as one. Eventually, most are known only by the name of their Knight suit, as though the warrior inside is no longer a separate entity.

Freeblade Knights tend to travel alone, or with only a small group of retainers or Sacristans. Often those Bondsmen who fought loyally beside a Noble while they were still part of a household will continue to do after their master becomes a Freeblade, their Armigers supporting the larger Knight as they did in the past. It is also not uncommon for Freeblades to band together – perhaps having been drawn to the same war zones during campaigns – forming lances that fight in much the same manner as a household detachment, but with a bond forged in battle alone. After achieving victory, such Freeblade groups typically disperse once more, although a few have been known to remain in each other's company for extended periods of time.

Regardless of their past tragedies or present company, and irrespective of the idiosyncrasies they develop after so long away from hearth and home, Freeblades still place great significance on acts of honour and duty, perhaps even more so than in their previous lives. Thus, wherever their travels may take them, a Freeblade Knight will fight to protect the citizens and soldiery of the Imperium and punish the foes of Mankind.

KALENA MAXUS, THE STORMWALKER

When the Great Rift tore its way across the galaxy, the Knight world of Kamador lay directly in its path. Engulfed by the billowing madness of the maelstrom, the planet was beset by tides of mutants, Heretic Astartes and daemonic abominations. Led by the garishly grotesque warriors of the Emperor's Children, the Chaos hordes tore down the strongholds of one Noble house after another. Though the Knights of Kamador fought furiously to defend their world, in the end they could not prevail. A single Noble escaped the devastation – Lady Kalena Maxus, the Stormwalker.

Kalena did not willingly flee the death of Kamador. Rather, she was commanded by High King Arturo to spread the word of her world's fall, and to exact revenge unending upon the forces of Chaos for their murderous deeds. This, Lady Maxus has done with a burdened heart ever since. She haunts the fringes of the Great Rift, rallying Imperial forces wherever she finds them and leading them to fight back against the heretical foe. The arrival of the Stormwalker has turned the tide of many battles, Lady Maxus dedicating each hard-won victory to the memory of her slain kinsmen.

AMARANTHINE

As most Freeblades maintain no house markings, and few show any sign of Imperial or Adeptus Mechanicus alignment, it can be difficult to ascertain their past. The lone Freeblade known as Amaranthine earned his name from the beleaguered Imperial defenders of Romaric VII. Most believe the name is a reference to the Knight's distinctive purple-red hull, but others claim it honours an Imperial saint.

Silent and purposeful, the Knight never replies to hails, vox transmissions or other attempts to converse with him. However, during the Tiberius Wars it was observed that the Knight complied with the voxed tactics of those he fought alongside, avoiding firing lines and vanquishing foes as per incoming requests. It led the defenders to believe that though he did not speak, he was always listening. Only invitations to stay once the battle was won seemed to go unheeded.

THE OBSIDIAN KNIGHT

Little is known about the Freeblade that some call the Obsidian Knight. The first recorded sighting came during the Damocles Gulf Crusade over two hundred years ago. Out of nowhere strode the dark behemoth, covered in fell symbols. He single-handedly halted a major T'au assault, and appeared in dozens of battles. The Knight disappeared by campaign's end, remembered only in legend. Two centuries later, when the legendary T'au Commander Shadowsun launched her invasion of Agrellan, the Obsidian Knight appeared once again. Whether or not it was the same Knight is unknown, but it fought with the same zeal, annihilating entire cadres of the enemy. Upon Prefectia, the Obsidian Knight stormed into battle against the largest battlesuits and artillery walkers the T'au Empire could deploy, scoring one engine-kill after another before he was finally brought low and driven into a vast geothermic pit. The Imperium recovered the Obsidian Knight's wreckage, believing his legend done. Yet later in that same campaign the Freeblade mysteriously retuned to the fight, as vehement as ever.

GERANTIUS, THE GREEN KNIGHT

Known as the Forgotten or Green Knight, Gerantius resides at the centre of Sacred Mountain, a blessed peak that rises from the heart of Alaric Prime's largest island. There is rumoured to be a vault of archeotech and lost lore there, over which he stands guard. Ancient and mysterious, Gerantius has defended the vault, and his world, since time immemorial. Whenever the planet is threatened, the Green Knight will rise from his slumber and march upon the enemies of Alaric Prime.

Rumours abound about the enigmatic figure, but the truth is that none know who or what the Green Knight is, as no one has ever spoken with the Noble that pilots it, if indeed there is anything inside to reply to their hails. All that is certain is that in times of need, the Green Knight arises to drive back the enemies of Alaric Prime with reaper chainsword and thermal cannon. Gerantius was pivotal to the victory over the Orks of the Red Waaagh!, and with cult uprisings occurring across Alaric Prime in the wake of the Great Rift, the Green Knight marches to battle once more.

ON ADAMANT THRONES

Even the smallest Noble household has a seat of power, whether it be a fortified tower upon an outlying moon, a slab-sided bastion looming over the house's fiefdom, mountaintop fastness, vacuum-resistant hab-dome, armoured cave-system or whatever else. The foundations of the largest and oldest of these sit upon the archeotech remains of the Long March ships themselves, deeply buried by the passing of millennia but still concealing secrets of ancient technology that the Noble houses guard jealously.

Within the throne room or audience chamber of each Noble house, its rulers hold court. Ranging from a single Baron and their direct courtiers, to vast assemblages of Nobles, Bondsmen, courtiers and more, these gatherings observe the endless rituals of their world, deal with matters of rulership for the common folk, and politick constantly amongst themselves. The figures involved in such internecine intrigues are many and varied, from sages and advisors to Imperial preachers, tech-magi, Sacristan representatives, house militia officers and countless others. While marriage and the continuation of the Noble bloodlines is often regulated by formal arranged pacts, many Knights join themselves romantically and politically to a consort. These individuals may be the daughters or sons of other Noble families, high-placed members of court, or even – in unusual cases – other Knights of a different or lesser rank. What matters more than their origin is their incisive minds, their skill at courtly politics, and their dedication to being a societal power behind their Noble's martial throne.

MANIFEST VENGEANCE

Once this dogged Freeblade sets his mind to the hunt, no force in the galaxy can stop him. Manifest Vengeance has tracked foes across entire sectors of the galaxy in order to land a killing blow with his chain-cleaver.

AURIC ARACHNUS

Wielding blade and battle cannon, the Knight known as Auric Arachnus fights against the Imperium's foes. With its distinctive bright yellow livery and contrasting stylised arachnid symbol, the bold Freeblade is designed to draw attention and the enemy's fire. From whence the Knight came there is no clue, nor does its pilot ever emerge. When the shadow of Hive Fleet Behemoth fell across the Ultima Segmentum, however, the legend of Auric Arachnus began. As Imperial armies rallied to repel the foe, the Knight Paladin was a tower of firepower, and when eventually overrun, its reaper blade scythed down swarms of foes. As the Tyranids pressed in upon the Ultramarines, the Chapter was forced back to its home world and Auric Arachnus travelled with them. There, the Freeblade earned great renown by slaying a Dominatrix.

THE WHITE WARDEN

Once, the Noble Neru Degallio was the ruler of House Degallio. His Knight, the White Warden, was a symbol of the power and influence of his extended family. All of that was lost when the Red Waaagh! descended upon his planet. As the most powerful knightly house on Alaric Prime, it fell to Degallio to weather the brunt of the fighting, and of all the house's Nobles, Neru alone survived the fierce fighting. In the wake of this pyrrhic victory, the lord of House Degallio found himself made a scapegoat by lesser houses seeking political gains. After the mysterious disappearance of his consort, Neru turned Freeblade, taking the name of his Knight and leaving Alaric Prime far behind. Since then, the White Warden has fought countless enemies of the Imperium, each time proving himself a superlative warrior and tactician. He has forged a strong bond with the courageous Space Marines of the Salamanders Chapter, in whom Degallio discovered a kindred desire to defend the common folk of the Emperor's realm. Since the opening of the Great Rift, the White Warden has risked his life repeatedly in defence of the Salamanders' home world of Nocturne.

A TAPESTRY OF GLORIES

For millennia the Imperial Knights have woven tales of heroism and chivalry across the stars. They have been the shield and the sword, defending Humanity and slaying the monsters that would threaten its reign. Though the darkness has closed in around them time and again, always the Knights drive it back, lighting the void with their courage and valour.

M15-M32 AGE OF HONOUR AND VENGEANCE

Foundations of the Knight Worlds
Standard Template Construct technology is created, heralding an era of discovery, innovation and expansion. Alongside the development of warp travel, STCs enable star-faring ships to voyage enormous distances swiftly, and transform the way that new planets are settled. The first Knight worlds are established by the colonists of the Long March ships.

Nightfall
Mankind is pitched into the self-inflicted turmoil of Old Night. The Knight worlds, insulated by their conservative cultures, endure as scattered motes of light in a sea of darkness.

Omnissiah Regnum
After centuries of isolation, Mars receives a visitation from the Emperor. Its peoples believe him to be the Omnissiah, god of all machines. It is Knights of House Taranis that first bend the knee to this deity from the void, an honour they will not soon forget. The Emperor and the Mechanicum's Fabricator General ratify the Mars Treaty, allying the Red Planet with Terra.

The First of Many
The Knight world of Chrysis is rediscovered and brought back into the wider fold of Humanity. Many more soon follow.

The Great Crusade
As the Emperor's crusading fleets sweep out across the galaxy, uniting Humanity's scattered worlds one by one, numerous knightly households are with them. It is a time of restoration and glory, in which many houses form strong ties to the Explorator fleets and Titan Legions of the Mechanicum. Others pledge their allegiance and strength to particular Primarchs or Imperial commanders. The Knights prove stalwart allies, the devastation they wreak more than compensating for their sometimes stilted or prickly ways, and it seems as though they will play an instrumental part in establishing the Imperium's dominance across the stars.

The Horus Heresy
Warmaster Horus plunges the Imperium into civil war. Corrupted by the Dark Gods of Chaos, he leads fully half the Space Marine Legions in open revolt. Some knightly houses join the rebels, either compelled by unbreakable oaths of fealty or tainted by the touch of Chaos. Many more Noble houses fight hard for the Imperium, winning one victory after another against the turncoat forces. On both sides, the bloodlines of a number of Noble houses are brought to an end during the incredibly fierce fighting, their lives callously expended in the name of victory.

The Traitors' Due
After Horus' defeat at the Siege of Terra, the surviving loyalists hound the traitor forces across the galaxy. Knights are at the forefront of many such campaigns, venting their disgust, hatred and outrage upon those Nobles that betrayed them. A higher number of Freeblades join the fighting, exacting revenge for houses lost and home worlds destroyed.

M33-M40 AGE OF BANNERS RAISED

Defence of Vorinth
A vast Ork Waaagh! descends upon the Knight world of Vorinth. Its Noble houses fight with courage and honour, but are hopelessly outnumbered, and no other Imperial forces can answer their call for aid in time. Though they break the back of the greenskin horde, the Knights of Vorinth are utterly wiped out. When their loss is recorded on Terra, the Bell of Lost Souls is tolled twice.

Long Awaited
After over half a century of self-imposed exile as Freeblades, the Agaron Brothers return to their home world of Silverdawn, where they are welcomed back as heroes.

The War of Recovery
Twelve knightly houses – including Taranis, Raven and Drakhs – send lances to join the Adeptus Mechanicus push into the Mortuam Chain System. Their efforts are highly successful, with ancient human technologies being wrested from a clutch of xenos warlords across the system.

Daemon Tide
Three Imperial sectors are overrun by a vast army of the immaterium referred fearfully to as the Daemon Tide. Deploying into the Daemons' path, five knightly houses – led by the renowned Nobles of Terryn – form an adamant bastion to halt the rampage. Using swift-loping packs of Armiger Helverins and Warglaives, High Queen Desmadara Terryn channels the Daemons through the shattered valleys of Godsmote. As the warp-born creatures spill onto the Hollow Plain they are subjected to thunderous bombardment by two dozen Knights Castellan. The Daemons' casualties are phenomenal, yet with no concept of fear they surge onward to exact revenge. Over six hundred Questoris-class Knights storm out to meet them, enduring barrages of sorcery, flame and filth that send towering Knight suits toppling in ruin.

With Queen Desmadara and her Exalted Court at the lance-point, the Knights slam into the still-vast daemonic horde. They carve a path of annihilation to its heart, the ground shaking beneath their tread, unclean ichor drenching their legs. Though empyric fiends and coruscating warp energies tear down one Knight after another, their momentum is unstoppable. At last, with reaper chainswords howling and thunderstrike gauntlets crackling, the Exalted Courts of three knightly houses engage the masters of the Daemon Tide.

The battle that follows is so grandiose and cataclysmic that it spawns a hundred songs, tales and tapestries. Several heroic Knights are slain by the enormous Great Unclean One Bolothrax, before the Knights Valiant known as Master of Iron and Fellbreaker successfully pinion the foul abomination with their thundercoil harpoons. With their quarry unable to move, the Knights hack the mighty Daemon apart.

Bolothrax's banishment spells the end for the Daemon Tide, though they wreak much more destruction before they finally fade back into the warp. It is on that day that Bolothrax's unending grudge against House Terryn and all its descendants is born.

The Clouds Part

The Imperium makes first contact with the Knight world of Kragh after the warp storms surrounding it – which had raged for over twenty millennia – finally abate.

Unexpected Silence

Facing bloody cult uprisings across the mining worlds of the Taurian Belt, Imperial Fists Captain Lynator calls upon the Knights of House Hawkshroud to lend their aid. To his shock, they fail to answer, one of only three times in recorded history that such a thing has happened.

The War of Six Crowns

In a convoluted war of honour, the High Monarchs of six Noble Great Houses battle one another for rule of the Sextant Stars. Despite warnings from the Adeptus Terra to cease this costly madness, the Knights persist in their war, ignoring all the sanctions that the Imperium dare apply.

Slaughter on the Fireplains

Amidst thundering geysers of geothermal flame, the Knights of House Raven confront and crush Waaagh! Smogbelcha on the Fireplains of Voth.

M40-M41 AGE OF BRACED GATES

Disaster on Nalibraxis II

During the Yoladrian Crusade, lances of House Cadmus Knights land on the swamp world of Nalibraxis II. The Knights march in support of Cadian infantry regiments deployed to that fog-shrouded world, only to be caught in a perfectly executed ambush by the forces of the Thousand Sons. Many Nobles are slain and Knight suits lost as sorcerous constructs and Daemon Engines close in from all sides. In the wake of the carnage, House Cadmus vows revenge, and spends the next three decades exacting it.

War for the Cage

The Diamor System is plunged into anarchy when a combined force of the Black Legion, Crimson Slaughter and Word Bearers launch a concerted attack. Though their invasion is system-wide, the true objective of the Chaos hosts is the Adeptus Mechanicus dig site on the world of Amethal.

A huge army of Imperial Knights, drawn from House Raven and many of the lesser houses that owe it fealty, fights in the Imperial counter-assault, over one hundred towering war engines facing off against Heretic Astartes and Renegade Titans. Though they suffer heavy casualties, the Nobles of House Raven remain undaunted. Empowered by their wrath, they storm the Chaos lines during the campaign's final battle, and are instrumental in bringing down the enemy's Titans and driving the Black Legion from Amethal for good. In the war's wake, House Raven strengthen their bonds of allegiance with both the Tech-Priests of forge world Metalica and the Blood Angels Space Marine Chapter.

Lone Guardian

Sir Yannil of House Derthos swears an oath to stand guard over the beset mining colonies on the moon of Tandosa. Enthroned within Tower of Strength, his Knight Castellan, Yannil sees off repeated attacks by Drukhari pirates. Outraged at the intervention by Yannil and his ironclad behemoth, the leaders of the Drukhari raiding parties send a force of swift gunships and agile fighter-craft to eliminate the impediment once and for all. Engaging his airborne tormentors as best he can, Yannil sends a missive to House Derthos for aid, then digs in and vows to hold his ground until he is relieved.

It is a week later that Knights of House Derthos reach Tandosa. They find Tower of Strength still standing, ravaged by energy blasts and explosives, its pilot clinging to life by a thread. Around him are scattered the wrecks of the Drukhari vessels, eliminated to the last.

An Error of Judgement

The Genestealer Cult of the Withering Worm attempt to infiltrate the Noble bloodline of House Belligerus. They quickly learn the magnitude of their mistake when the conditioning of the Nobles' Thrones aids them in resisting the broodmind, though not without great

struggle. In a single night of fire and violence, the cult cells are driven into the open and exterminated like vermin by Belligerus' Knights.

The Red Waaagh!

With the aid of the ferocious battle-brothers of the Space Wolves Chapter, the Knight world of Alaric Prime defeats the greenskin hordes of the Red Waaagh! The price of victory is steep, however, and a veil of Inquisitorial secrecy is drawn over the dire events that mark the war's culmination.

Betrayal on Donatos

The knightly houses of Adrastapol launch a crusade to save the industrial world of Donatos from heretic forces. Five Noble houses deploy their lances, led by High King Tolwyn of House Draconis, yet disaster strikes after Houses Chimaeros and Wyvorn – their Thrones Mechanicum tainted through Chaos witchery – turn upon their allies in a bloody betrayal.

With the High King dead and the knightly forces in disarray, it falls to the young Sire Danial Tan Draconis to rally Houses Draconis, Pegasson and Minotos. Uniting the planet's scattered Imperial forces, the Knights launch a determined fight back, seeking vengeance upon the traitorous Nobles and the Word Bearers both.

The Fall of Phodiam

A tendril of Hive Fleet Leviathan engulfs the hive world of Phodiam. Due to warp storm activity, the Imperial relief force is lost, leaving Phodiam defenceless. Into the breach steps a company of Freeblades calling themselves the Tarnished Shield, seven exiled warriors led by Ferrum Magnificat. Through selfless sacrifice and heroic effort, the Freeblades hold the Tyranid swarms at bay long enough for over a third of the planet's populace to evacuate successfully.

Storm of Shadows

Warp storms rage across the galaxy. Dozens of Noble houses despatch Knights to help defend the Cadian Gate, Taranis and Raven foremost amongst them, but even their might is not enough to prevent Cadia's fall. House Astropaths cry out in horror at the omens of impending doom. Bastion fleets are recalled to their parent Knight worlds, racing for safe anchorage before the storm hits. Everywhere the Nobles see signs of Old Night's return, bracing against the opening of the Great Rift and the appalling carnage that follows.

M41 AGE OF HONOUR ENDURING

Indomitus

As the Astronomican flares back to life, it illuminates a riven and beset Imperium. Primarch Guilliman declares his Indomitus Crusade, setting out to pierce the darkness of the Imperium Nihilus and drive back the resurgent forces of Chaos. House Taranis proudly pledges all but a fraction of its fighting strength to the endeavour, waking their oldest Knight suits from slumber and deploying their greatest relics of archeotech to aid in the fight.

The Great Cull

On Raisa, the number of mutants lurking in the forests explodes exponentially beneath the baleful light of the Siren's Storm. As the heretical hordes swell they spill across the land, destroying agriplexes and settlements at will. Baron Roland declares a cull to end all culls, marching out from Swinford Hall at the head of his entire household. Weeks of slaughter follow, and the lives of many proud Knights and courageous Sacristans are lost before the mutants are finally driven back. They leave behind mountains of dead so high that the pall from blazing corpse pyres shrouds Raisa in smoke. House Cadmus raises new fortifications to overlook the deepest woodlands, even more wary now of the dangers that lurk beneath their boughs.

Iron and Fire

The Knights of Tanika march to the aid of the Iron Hands Chapter on Medusa. Led by the matriarchal huntresses of House Thorne, they battle against the Renegade Titans of the Legio Abominator and buy time for the Iron Hands' Clans to rally and fight back. Forging steely chains of allegiance and loyalty, the Iron Hands and Tanikan Knights drive the heretic invaders back.

Rise of the Chainbreaker

Surging from amidst the storms of the Great Rift, Warsmith Ghanshor's Iron Warriors subjugate the Knight world of Randoryn Alpha. Amidst the horrors of the occupation, the Knight suit known as Canis Rex stirs to life and frees its Noble pilot, Sir Hekhtur, from imprisonment. As the last surviving loyal warrior of House Cerberan, Hekhtur swears the Freeblade oath before setting about rescuing as many enslaved Randorynians as he can. Sir Hekhtur and Canis Rex escape the world alive, and the Noble vows to wage an endless war of vengeance against the forces of Chaos.

War on Every Front

Cries for help pour into the astropathic relays of Kolossi. With stoic determination, the rulers of House Raven despatch one lance after another, sending their Noble warriors out into the void aboard Mechanicus Explorator ships and war barges, many never to return. The House's Sacristans cogitate that, at the current rate of deployment, Raven will have fully emptied the Vault Transcendent within one anno-cycle.

Xenostorm

House Mortan recall their questing lances as word reaches them of a vast Ork Waaagh! on a collision course with their home world of Kimdaria. Rather than wait for Waaagh! Ragrat to fall upon them, the Knights of Mortan elect to hunt the greenskin horde as they would a single monstrous beast. So begins a bloody war across three systems, with lances of Mortan Knights bolstering planetary garrisons and attempting to bait, slow and divide the Orks until they can be wiped out once and for all.

Daemonic Vengeance

Amidst the swirling fury of the Damocles Gulf, High King Tybalt leads the Knights of House Terryn in their latest push against the T'au invaders. They strike at the recently reclaimed T'au colony world of Shans'et, formerly an Imperial-held planet known as Gossamehr. Initially, the Terryn offensive progresses well. The Knights are supported by a force of Raven Guard Space Marines, who scout ahead of their advance and repeatedly negate the xenos enemy's rapid-manoeuvre tactics.

The battle takes an unexpected turn, however, as the skies curdle into matted filth and black rain falls, rotting all that it touches. From the sucking morass rise the Daemons of Nurgle, led by the bloated abomination that is Bolothrax the Great Unclean One. In the vicious conflict that follows, House Terryn sustains terrible losses, while the vengeful Bolothrax wounds High King Tybalt sorely and fells the Knights of three of his closest blood relatives.

It is only when the Raven Guard lure the T'au forces into contact with the daemonic host that Tybalt's Exalted Court are able to spearhead a breakout. The mauled Imperial forces stage a fighting retreat to their extraction point, battling droning plague creatures all the way. They leave Shans'et to the frustrated Daemons, who waste no time in making the T'au suffer.

The Malefica Crusade

The fanatically pious House Thale empty the keeps of their home world, Glorifica, to launch a witch-hunting crusade across the Segmentum Pacificus.

The Saviours' Hunt

Amidst the darkness of the Imperium Nihilus, the factory world of Drakkatoria is struck by a reality disjunction. Tides of horrifying shadow-spawn crawl from the nether-realm of Aelindrach and infest every city on the globe. Perpetual night falls, and murderous Mandrakes and wraith-creatures hunt the terrified populace through the dark, led by the fiendish Kheradruakh the Decapitator. Drakkatoria's Astropaths scream their minds bloody as they cry out for aid. Though it costs them their lives, their pleas do not go unanswered.

The bastion ships of House Griffith arrive in orbit. Their heavy landers surge down through the shadow-choked atmosphere, disgorging hunting lances by the dozen into Drakkatoria's nightmarish urban sprawl. The campaign that follows is a vicious affair. Griffith Armigers sweep through the industrial ruins, banishing the shadows with their hull-lumen and using their weapons to flush out packs of Mandrakes into the guns of the larger Knights. Hissing nightmares emerge impossibly within the cockpits of Knight suits, knifing screaming Nobles to death in frenzies of violence. Brave Sacristans pilot their landers into the darkest zones, lighting vast brazier circles to drive back the shadows and the terrors that lurk within them.

The tide finally turns when a trio of Dominus-class Griffith Knights manage to forge a path to the shattered webway spar that began the madness, and subject it to sustained bombardment. Sensing the link to their dark dimension closing, those shadow creatures still able to retreat do so, returning to Aelindrach. Those that cannot slink into the darkest depths they can find, fleeing the return of dawn on Drakkatoria.

House Griffith claim victory over the battered ruins of the industrial cities, though the planet's populace will never sleep soundly again.

Against the Storm

Hastoria II faces a daemonic apocalypse as the coils of Warp Storm Baphomet engulf it. Yet the planet's Novamarines and Cadian defenders receive aid unlooked for when the Freeblade known as the Stormwalker arrives. Supported by the Knight Castellan's massive guns, protected by its crackling shields, the Imperial forces stage a determined stand that at last halts the Daemons before the Shrine of Saint Hastus.

A Time for Vengeance

Far from being dismayed at the sudden ascendancy of Chaos, House Krast relishes this chance to take revenge upon their hated foes. No less than six Crusades of Vengeance are launched from Chrysis, spearing through the void towards the forge worlds of Voss, Phaeton, Urdesh, Stygies, Artemia Majoris and distant Graia. As they link up with Adeptus Mechanicus forces, Krast's bloodthirsty crusades gather pace, driving the traitors before them.

Debts Long Owed

Already stretched dangerously thin, House Hawkshroud find themselves in deadly peril as the Orks of Waaagh! Zagsmasha descend upon their home world of Krastellan. Cries for help are sent, debts long owed called in at last from the many allies that Hawkshroud have so selflessly aided over the millennia. Most fall upon deaf ears, but on Baal, Valhalla and Dragon's End, relief forces begin to muster, while in the empyrean, the Primaris Marines of the Valiant Blades turn their ships' helms towards Krastellan. Whether these reinforcements will arrive before the home world of House Hawkshroud is overrun remains to be seen.

Here be Dragons

The Questor Mechanicus world of Altevfor is ravaged by fire-breathing packs of Heldrakes that swoop through its polluted atmosphere and wreak havoc amongst its manufactorums. Princeps Adalace orders the attacks ended, and her Sacristans use their macro-cogitators to determine that the Heldrakes are striking from the mountaintop forge-temple of Gammapeak.

Princeps Adalace mobilises her Exalted Court and the vast majority of her world's Knights, and leads a determined attack up the slopes of the mountain. The Knights discover hundreds of mechanical dragons roosting amidst the ruined forge-temple, and for days the smog clouds that wreathe the mountain are lit by flame and gunfire. When finally the Princeps and her much reduced knightly lances march back down the mountainside, the Heldrakes are no more.

The War of Death's Welcome

A splinter fleet of Hive Fleet Hydra ploughs down upon the Knight world of Death's Welcome. Morbid nihilists who worship the Emperor as the harbinger of war and ending, the houses of Death's Welcome greet the Tyranid invasion not with terror, but sombre rituals of celebration. Marching out in Knight suits of sable and bone, singing dirges from beneath their chain mail veils, the Knights of Houses Drudge, Fervans and Scythe prepare to meet their long-foretold end.

The war is spectacularly violent, with tidal waves of Tyranid beasts crashing against the Knights' lines. The Nobles' guns reap thousands of xenos by the minute, only for the next wave to scramble atop the bodies of the fallen and hurl themselves at the Knights in turn. Rippers slither in rivers up the legs of Knight suits to gnaw through hydraulic cables and clog workings with their corpses. Hormagaunts and Termagants erode the Knights' armour plating through sheer weight of bioshot and claw, and then tear and stab at vital systems. All across the battlefield Knights are lost, falling into an endless writhing sea of xenos creatures.

Yet still the Knights of Death's Welcome fight on, their hymnals growing ever louder and more fervent as the end approaches. Against all expectation, the surviving Nobles find the Tyranid tide ebbing, then drying up altogether. Hydra's bio-ships flee orbit, their reserves of biomass dangerously spent. Just eighteen Nobles remain alive from a starting force of over four hundred, yet through their survival, Death's Welcome also endures.

A Claim Denied

Aeldari raiders from Craftworld Alaitoc launch a sudden, shocking assault upon Voltoris, the home world of House Terryn. The cause of this aggression is unclear, but the response is swift. Alongside the famous Chainbreaker, the Knights of House Terryn fight to drive the xenos from their world. Casualties are heavy on both sides, but it is the will of the Aeldari that breaks first.

For the Omnissiah

Though they are of Imperial alignment, the knightly houses of Avarris launch a stinging assault across the Vidar Sector to relieve the heretical siege of forge world Triplex Phall.

The Ancients Awaken

What begins as an isolated conflict between the Adeptus Mechanicus and the Necrons on the quarry world of Amontep II becomes a galaxy-wide war. Across the planets of both the Adeptus Mechanicus and the Knights, Necron presence is suddenly and startlingly revealed. The mountains of Auros IV rumble with tectonic tremors as Necron tombs awaken beneath the surface of House Vulker's fiefdoms. On Voltoris, the recently healed High King Tybalt recalls swathes of his house's Knights from the Eastern Fringe, jeopardising their chances of winning an ongoing war against the T'au Empire to counter an emergent Necron threat upon Terryn's home world. Dozens of forge worlds issue calls for reinforcement from their satellite Knight worlds as Necron tombs stir to life beneath their foundations, yet the Noble houses are equally beset. Many believe that the Necron awakening has accelerated as a response to the coming of the Great Rift, but whatever the truth of the matter, well over half of all the Imperium's forge and Knight worlds are now besieged by the ancient race.

Renegades of Dharrovar

Sir Drantar of House Taranis is sent to hunt down, once and for all, the lunatic Knight known as Litany of Destruction. Drantar and his Knight Red Might follow the trail of auto-infectious madness that spreads in the Litany's wake, their hunt taking them to the Nachmund Gauntlet, and the contested world of Dharrovar. The world is home to the traitorous Knights of House Mandrakor, and it is there, amidst constant Knight wars, that Red Might and the Litany of Destruction clash at last…

Upon the war-torn world of Agrellan, the Freeblade known as the Obsidian Knight led the charge into the battle lines of the T'au Empire. Though the pernicious aliens employed their most heretical technomantic trickery, and though one proud Imperial champion after another met a glorious end, still the Obsidian Knight fought tirelessly on.

ARMIGER WARGLAIVES

Nimble and responsive, Armiger Warglaives lope towards the enemy with purposeful strides. On one arm they wield fearsome reaper chain-cleavers, their adamantium teeth whirring, their actuator motors roaring. On the other arm they bear menacing thermal spears, bulky melta weapons that are essentially stripped down equivalents of the Knight Errant's thermal cannon. A single shot from such a weapon can vaporise even the most heavily protected combatant, melt through the wall of a bunker or reduce a battle tank to a molten wreck. Atop their carapace, each Warglaive also carries a heavy stubber for reaping infantry, or else a meltagun that augments their already fearsome anti-armour capabilities.

Though they are the lightest class of Imperial Knight regularly deployed to the battlefields of the 41st Millennium, each Armiger is still an imposing war engine capable of butchering entire squads. They possess exceptional speed, able to outpace most battle tanks and transport vehicles when moving at a flat-out run, and react almost as quickly as a flesh-and-blood warrior. Moreover, to compensate for their comparatively smaller size, Armiger-class Knights typically hunt in packs of two or three. In the case of Warglaives, this involves rapidly outflanking and encircling their quarry like wolves on the prowl, before closing in on a rune-transmitted signal to trap and slaughter the enemy.

Unusually for Knights, Armigers are not fitted with a full Throne Mechanicum. Instead they are controlled using a more compact device known as a Helm Mechanicum. Placed upon the head and connected via pre-frontal sockets to the pilot's cerebrum, these machines do not require a full Becoming ritual in order for neural interfacing to be successful. For this reason, the prestige of piloting an Armiger is significantly less than that attached to sitting a fully fledged Throne Mechanicum. This is compounded by the fact that, while Armigers can operate independently, it is traditional for their Helms Mechanicum to be neurally slaved to the command impulses of a larger Knight, rendering them subordinate. To accept such mental serfdom is to possess the rank of Bondsman, and while this is certainly no mark of dishonour, it is far from glorious.

It is for these reasons that the piloting of Armigers falls to those from the lower social strata of the Noble houses. Some give this duty to distant relatives and minor offshoots of more established bloodlines, or the surviving Knights of a house that has fallen upon hard times. Others elevate the finest common-born warriors from amongst their household guard or planetary militia forces, raising their families' standing from mere peasantry to valued and respected meritocracy. Still other Noble houses maintain specialist sub-orders of favoured retainers who are fated from birth to be Armiger pilots. Such is the case with House Griffith's Order of the Hound, who are inculcated with notions of faithful service and honourable submission to a Noble's will. These warriors are expert Armiger pilots who favour the close-quarters aggression of the Warglaive, and who stride into battle alongside their masters filled with dogged determination to do their betters proud.

ARMIGER HELVERINS

The Armiger Helverin is a fast-moving weapons platform designed to lay down blistering hails of heavy fire while running rings around the enemy's forces. In place of the close-ranged armaments of the Warglaive, each Helverin bears a pair of Armiger autocannons. Capable of firing hundreds of armour piercing shells per minute, even a single such weapon can swiftly whittle down infantry ranks or shred lightly armoured vehicles. With Helverins mounting two of these formidable weapons each, and hunting in packs up to three Knights strong, their withering fusillades can rapidly break an army's flank or blunt the foe's assault well before it can hit home.

Helverins also mount carapace weaponry in the same fashion as Warglaives. Many favour heavy stubbers for their simple application in adding to the Helverin's already formidable weight of fire. However, other Bondsmen will choose – or have their betters choose for them – to mount carapace meltaguns on their Helverins, thus providing them with short-range punch should the enemy's armour or elite infantry move in too close.

> '*Through faith, acceptance. Through acceptance, obedience. Through obedience, honour. Through honour, chivalry. Through chivalry, glory eternal.*'
>
> *- The Bondsman's Motto*

For many Armiger pilots, the mental imperatives transmitted through their neural bonds can feel unnatural and invasive. It is common for new pilots to feel a sense of resentment or upset at having their desires and opinions directed remotely, while those without the requisite mental fortitude may even lose their grip on their sense of self. More than one Freeblade has been born from such feelings, the Armiger pilot rebelling and fleeing rather than enduring the mental dominance of another.

It is for this reason that many Armiger pilots train at the side of a Knight Preceptor before assuming their duties alongside their bond-liege. The dutiful and heroic example set by the Knights Preceptor inspires Armiger pilots to accept their subservience to such obvious champions of the Imperium, and also plants within their minds a firm aspiration to do their duty and to live up to the example set for them.

Even as the Knights Preceptor are conditioning the Armiger pilots, they are also busy assessing their abilities. Most Bondsmen begin piloting from the helm of a Warglaive, for its weapons and role are both relatively straightforward. Those who demonstrate a cool nerve and a marksman's eye are soon recommended by the Knight Preceptor for promotion to a Helverin.

Helverin packs are able to serve a number of strategic roles upon the field of battle. From laying down enfilading fire and forcing dug-in enemies from their positions, to guarding a Knight army's flanks from aircraft and light armour, to escort or scouting missions in hostile territory, Armiger Helverins are versatile and highly destructive war engines. Small wonder that they are popular throughout both Imperial and Adeptus Mechanicus Noble houses, and relied upon heavily to support their larger compatriots at war.

Bondsman Voss worked his Armiger's controls, slowing the Helverin's strides as he rounded the corner of the ruined manufactorum. Gnarled trees and scrubby growths scraped at his steed's hull as he forged a path through the thicket and emerged at the end of the Processional of Heroes. Some three hundred yards ahead lay the heretics' left flank, traitor militia and artillery tanks dug in behind prepared barricades. They were firing furiously, directing a massive weight of fire against the Hawkshroud Knights trying to forge a path up Conveyance Route Beta.

Bondsman Kiele's Helverin appeared through the undergrowth to Voss' rear. The two Armiger pilots flashed confirmation runes to one another via their data-manifolds. Choral designators chimed through Voss' cockpit.

'Lady Sorenica,' voxed Voss. 'We are in position, my lady. We await your command.'

'Have the heretics seen you, Bondsman?' came the haughty voice of his bond-liege.

'Negative, my lady,' said Voss. 'The traitors are too busy firing at your lance to watch their flanks.'

Sorenica didn't deign to reply vocally. Instead, Voss felt a tingle through his Helm Mechanicum, and an overriding desire to attack at once rose within his mind. This was his lady's imperative, he knew, but it felt like his own, an appealing notion synonymous with honour through fealty. Accelerating his Knight to a purposeful stride, Voss flipped his targeters into place and roused the spirits of his autocannons. It was time to do his duty.

KNIGHTS ERRANT

The Errant is one of the most common classes of Knight suit. It forms a mainstay of knightly forces across the Imperium, and has remained an enduringly popular design for millennia.

Knights Errant are best used as aggressive, mid-to-close-range assault platforms. Pounding into battle at the vanguard, these war engines excel at hunting enemy tanks, walkers and monstrous beasts, especially amidst the tangled terrain of cityscapes, jungles and the like. This is thanks in no small part to the hideously destructive capabilities of their traditional primary armaments: the thermal cannon and reaper chainsword.

The thermal cannon is amongst the largest melta weapons in use by Imperial forces. Powered by massive thermo-inductor coils, these weapons project hissing columns of super-agitated microwaves that can reduce a tank to molten slag in a heartbeat or melt clean through an enemy bastion. Thermal cannons are especially effective at close range, where they pack such a phenomenal punch that anything smaller than a Titan is likely to be obliterated with a single shot. Even those not caught directly in the blast of these fearsome weapons fare little better, the air catching fire and swiftly reducing them to blazing husks.

The reaper chainsword is a shorter-ranged armament still, built to be wielded at close quarters much as an armed man would wield a blade – but what a blade it is. It is so long that it can be rammed through one side of a tank's hull and clean out the other. Its diamond-hard cutting teeth are driven by sanctified turbo-actuator engines, and can lop the arm from a combat walker or saw a vehicle in half with ease. Any living victim luckless enough to be struck by this weapon comes apart with explosive force, reduced to a blizzard of blood and gristle in the blink of an eye.

Knights Errant often mount pintle heavy stubbers or meltaguns that allow them to rain down still more death from on high. Some augment their strategic versatility through the mounting of secondary carapace weapon systems, while the most aggressive Noble pilots may even insist their reaper is replaced with a thunderstrike gauntlet. These slab-like crackling fists can backhand a Gorkanaut from its feet with a solid blow, or hurl enemy tanks across the battlefield like children's toys. Whatever their armaments, Knights Errant typically plunge into the fiercest front-line fighting. Thus, after battle, it is common to see them swarming with Sacristans, artisans labouring to repair the bellicose war engines' battle damage before the next engagement.

KNIGHTS PALADIN

No matter whether the enemy engages at short range or long, or if they send tanks, infantry or rampaging monsters into battle, the Knight Paladin has the versatility and might to face any threat. This Knight is designed to provide a strategic backbone for any lance, and – though it may not be as specialised towards a certain form of combat in the manner of other Questoris patterns – the Paladin is a traditional favourite amongst nearly every Noble house.

The signature weapon of the Knight Paladin is the rapid-fire battle cannon. A heavy, direct-firing artillery gun that spits a pair of shells at its target in quick succession, this weapon's concentrated double-salvoes ensure a very high shot-to-confirmed-kill ratio. The distinctive thump-thump sound of these cannons firing is so iconic that amongst certain Astra Militarum regiments – those that have fought alongside these Knights – it has become habit to wish 'the twinned thunder' upon hated foes.

So prevalent are the Knights Paladin amongst the Noble houses that it is a rare lance that does not include at least one. House Hawkshroud has long referred to their Paladins as the 'soul' of their knightly hosts, while amongst the ranks of House Vulker they are referred to simply as 'Optimals'. Although Paladins are sometimes piloted by younger Knights just out of their Becoming, such novitiate pilots are more often entrusted with a simple and effective Knight Errant. Paladins, by comparison, are usually the steeds of seasoned Nobles whose experience allows them to get the most out of these adaptable and effective Knight suits.

TO SAIL THE VOID

When fighting to defend their own worlds, the speed and manoeuvrability of Knights is usually sufficient to get them to where they are needed, but when they take the fight to foes on other planets the Nobles must use transports to reach their designated war zone. Some Knight worlds, especially those of an Imperial bent, maintain their own fleets of transport and combat cruisers, often former Imperial Navy craft. Others – including the vast majority of Questor Mechanicus Knight worlds – instead utilise Explorator craft and mass conveyance barges provided by an allied forge world. These ships ferry Nobles, Knight suits, Sacristans, attendant household servants, courtiers, bondsmilitia or whoever else to war, often alongside the towering engines of the Legios Titanicus or massed maniples of cyborg Skitarii. Different Knight worlds also approach combat drops in different ways. Though most Noble houses deploy their Knights using heavy haulers and mass transports, there are some that employ armoured drop-keeps for the task, which also allow them to maintain auxiliary air forces of Lightning and Thunderbolt fighters to clear landing zones, or – in the case of the Mechanicus-aligned House Faustiaris – make use of huge and ancient teleportariums that beam their Knight suits straight into battle amidst coronae of crackling lightning.

KNIGHTS WARDEN

The Knight Warden is a versatile and highly destructive weapons platform. Its standard ranged armament is the avenger gatling cannon, a dauntingly huge multi-barrelled firearm that can spit hundreds of foot-long armour-piercing shells per minute.

The avenger's phenomenal rate of fire and underslung heavy flamer means the Warden is well suited to an anti-infantry role, while also making it the bane of light, fast-moving vehicles such as bikes or transports. Wardens also mount a reaper chainsword or thunderstrike gauntlet to engage enemies at close quarters, while careful selection of carapace weapons also increases their ability to annihilate enemy battle tanks or even aircraft.

In many Noble houses, Knights Warden are reserved for the most accomplished pilots, often highly respected and veteran Barons or members of the Exalted Court. In part, this is because the Knight Warden traditionally has an especially strong-willed and belligerent machine spirit, making it a difficult steed to master. Knights Warden can be given to sudden and impulsive acts of selfless aggression on the battlefield, especially when around human allies or defenceless civilians, and they must be kept on a tight mental leash in order for their pilots to get the best from them.

'Trust ye in firepower, but keep thine reaper ready.'
— *Knight Warden maxim*

The comparative difficulty of piloting a Knight Warden makes them something of a status symbol amongst many Noble houses. A number of already accomplished Nobles have risen to true hero status while piloting a Knight Warden, with partnerships such as Sir Guillaume Terryn and Honourium, Lady Polena El Thorne and her Warden Death Inescapable, and Baron Isaac of Raven and the mighty Reaper of Lives all famed far beyond their own home worlds. Equally, the elite reputation of the Knight Warden is what makes the Avenger Lances of House Terryn – each consisting of a trio of Knights Warden armed with gatling cannons and thunderstrike gauntlets – appear especially impressive. That, and the complete devastation they invariably leave in their wake.

Ork warbands, Tyranid assault swarms and even the massed guerilla infantry of the Genestealer Cults – all melt away like tallow before a blowtorch when the Knights Warden open fire. Not only has this led to the widespread use of these suits by houses whose territories lie in the path of xenos invasions, but it is also responsible for the large number of Freeblades piloting Knights Warden. Often the sole survivors of once-mighty Knight worlds, these scarred Nobles escaped the fate of their kinsmen thanks to the exceptional firepower of their Knight suits, and now turn that same martial might to never-ending quests for revenge.

KNIGHTS GALLANT

Impetuous. Mad. Beyond bellicose. These words and more have been used to describe Knights Gallant, for they are considered by the majority of Nobles to be the most reckless and combative of all Imperial Knights. Pilot and machine share the same traits – they are aggressive, bold and difficult, if not impossible, to restrain. They long to attack, and will do so with unrelenting fervour.

To this end, Knights Gallant are armed almost exclusively for close combat, typically wielding a reaper chainsword and a thunderstrike gauntlet. This combination of weapons renders them especially ferocious when engaging the enemy's war engines and monstrous beasts; with every swing, the reaper is more than capable of scything the head from a Tyranid bio-

horror or running through the heaviest T'au Empire battlesuit. Meanwhile, a single good punch is all the thunderstrike gauntlet needs to kill almost anything smaller than a Titan, annihilating it in a searing flare and resonant boom.

Although geared towards close combat, the Knight Gallant does bear a single ball turret mounted weapon, either a heavy stubber or meltagun. As this is the Gallant's only ranged armament, pilots tend to use it in an opportunistic fashion, surprising their enemies with a sudden burst of lethal firepower in the moment before their charge slams home.

A Noble destined to pilot a Knight Gallant will learn three basic tenets when their Throne is installed within their steed. Depending upon the specific Knight household or the ancient heritage of the Throne, these commandments might be phrased in many different ways, but they all boil down to the same three truisms: trust in your ion shield, make all speed toward the foe, and strike swift and sure. Knights Gallant therefore waste no time in surging into the fight, their pounding strides eating up the distance between them and the foe with terrifying speed, their shields flickering as they absorb the enemy's increasingly panicked fire.

When a lance of Knights Gallant takes the battlefield, it is sure to attract a disproportionate amount of the enemy's firepower. Indeed, most foes will do anything they can in the hopes of preventing the Knights from reaching the front lines. Since the Great Crusade there have been many tales of the devastation wrought by these aggressive Knights, for their bold and reckless attacks have made them famous across the galaxy. It was a Knight Gallant that charged the vaunted heretic stronghold of Archeonite, smashing its way through thirteen defensive lines to batter down the citadel's gates. It was a trio of Knights Gallant that counter-attacked the Tyranid invasion of Grodisphere – ploughing headlong into a siege-breaking line of Carnifexes, blunting that xenos offensive in a spectacularly bloody fashion. Indeed, the great conqueror Solar Macharius is said to have favoured the Gallant Lance formation above all others for breaking enemy lines and bringing a swift end to attritional battles.

KNIGHTS CRUSADER

...nding the optimal firing position, the ...ight Crusader locks down its motive ...uators in preparation to unleash a ...nishing salvo. From its avenger gatling ...nnon it levels a fusillade of heavy shells, ...tching deadly patterns across the enemy ...ny's frontage. Its other weapon – a ...ermal cannon – causes the very air to ...zle as it fires blasts capable of reducing ...quad of Chaos Terminators to bubbling ...g with a single shot. With each section ...he battlefield it clears of foes, the ...usader's steady advance brings new ...gets under its sights, and it continues to ...leash destruction with every stride.

...e priority for a Knight Crusader is to ...d wide-open fields of fire, and if the ...ble pilot gives any concern to his own ...elter, it is but an afterthought. Each such ...rrior has long ago learned to trust in ...e strength of his Crusader's ion shield, ...d his own skill in positioning it to halt ...e worst of any incoming firepower. ...ould the enemy press forwards too ...sely, the Knight Crusader bears a heavy ...bber to thin their ranks, in addition ...the considerable crushing power of its ...mping feet.

...me Knights Crusader opt for a longer-...nged weapon, exchanging their thermal ...nnon for the rapid-fire battle cannon. ...ouse Raven has been known to employ ...ormation of Knights equipped in this ...nner, a deadly grouping known as an ...adicator Lance that can pulverise enemy ...ttle lines at a great distance, saturating ...em with high explosives. When deployed ...ongside one or more Knights Valiant, this ...mbination can provide a Noble house ...th phenomenal ranged killing power, ...sily equal to that of an Astra Militarum

The already impressive firepower of the Knight Crusader is further enhanced by its choice of carapace mounted weapon. Those that are equipped with Icarus autocannons on their shoulders are given an additional duty: to protect their comrades from airborne attack. Swivelling in response to their predictive auto-auguries, the Icarus cannons spit streams of flakk fire into the skies, barrels recoiling with each thumping shot. No matter how they jink and roll, enemy aircraft cannot long evade these raking streams of death, and are soon sent spiralling from the air aflame to detonate in distant fireballs beyond the horizon.

Alternatively, many Knights Crusader carry one of two types of missile rack upon their carapace. Those that bear an ironstorm missile pod into battle gain the ability to bombard infantry from afar, raining down terrifying hails of anti-personnel explosives. The wide radius and lethality of these munitions makes the ironstorm an exceptional weapon for decimating ranks of light infantry through sustained and merciless bombardment.

By comparison, the stormspear rocket pod is intended to provide a Knight with additional anti-armour capability. Perfect for slaughtering elite infantry or fast-moving battle tanks whose weapons may present a real threat to the Crusader or its fellows, stormspear rockets fire off in rapid volleys, emitting a distinctive, high-pitched scream before hitting home with hammerblow force.

Knights Crusader are typically piloted by especially dutiful and selfless Nobles. Though there are, of course, examples of high-ranking Barons and members of Exalted Courts piloting them, these machines are more often the steeds of those vassals who are of an especially humble or pious nature. Rather than seek the glory of the close-quarters kill, these warriors look only to defend their kin, to cover their glorious charge into battle and ensure that unseen threats are annihilated before they can besmirch the magnificence of their illustrious household. For this reason, the pilots of Knights Crusader are well respected by those within their house and without, seen as loyal and dependable comrades who will never be derelict in

KNIGHTS PRECEPTOR

The Knight Preceptor is a Questoris-class close-ranged powerhouse. Its design is intended to exemplify the core tenets of the Code Chivalric in battle: close with the enemy to an honourable range, engage them with sufficient force to show respect for their fortitude, and kill them quickly and cleanly in the Emperor's name. To this end, the Knight Preceptor is armed with a roaring reaper chainsword or crackling thunderstrike gauntlet, and the rare and terrifying laser cannon known as the las-impulsor. These weapons are best wielded at such close quarters that a Noble can look their enemy in the eye even as they slay them.

The las-impulsor is a ferociously powerful gun that, while comparatively short ranged for such sizeable ordnance, is more than capable of bringing a heretic fortress down in ruins or scything the leg from under an enemy Titan with a single concentrated salvo. The weapon works by building up an enormous charge of energy within capacitor shrines before cascading it down poly-sanctified conduits in escalating pulses. The result is a lightning-fast and devastating volley of laser blasts that can strip force shields from enemy war engines one at a time, and hammer their way through even the thickest armour or chitin to annihilate the vital systems beneath.

As an exemplar of knightly combat doctrines, the Preceptor is most often piloted by the arms-masters or precepts of the Noble houses. Grizzled veterans who have lived through decades of warfare, it is the job of these Nobles to set an example to their fellows, and to train their lessers in the arts of war. When not in battle it is their duty to train young squires in the skills they will require to pilot a Knight, and to instil the mental fortitude their wards will need to endure the Ritual of Becoming. The pilots of

Knights Preceptor are therefore figures viewed with equal amounts of fear and respect by those of their house, with even Barons of the Exalted Court speaking respectfully to the steely-eyed war dogs who taught them to fight.

It also falls to the arms-masters to recruit, train and mentally prepare the Bondsmen who pilot Armigers, the better to ensure that stable neural links are maintained and no act of dishonourable defiance occurs. As part of these duties, Knights Preceptor often take to the battlefield with one or more pairs of Helverins or Warglaives loping at their side. Some precepts form such strong neural choirs with their Bondsmen that they become permanent fighting units, acting as one with near-perfect synchronicity. Yet even those Armiger pilots who only serve for a short while under a precept are inevitably inspired by their feats of heroism, finding it easier to see the honour in their duty and submit willingly to the neural imperatives of their betters.

Most Knight Preceptor pilots seek to set an example upon the field of battle by hunting down and besting the largest and most fearsome enemies. This is a role well suited to the close-ranged lethality of their steeds, and one that the machine spirits of the Knight suits themselves relish. Countless battles have been turned in the Imperium's favour by the actions of a Knight Preceptor, marching fearlessly through hails of enemy fire before unleashing the screaming fury of its las-impulsor even as its flanking Armigers add their own firepower to the punishing salvo. Such an attack is more than all but the most resilient of enemies can survive, and even they last only long enough for the Preceptor to draw back its melee armament and finish the fight with a single thunderous blow.

LAS-IMPULSORS

Twice during the Imperium's history has the technology to create las-impulsors been thought lost. In the era of the Great Crusade, the weapons were produced solely upon a trio of forge worlds that were famed for their skill in creating and innovating laser weapons. These planets, known collectively as the Deuterium Stars, possessed the secrets of fusion fire, and their tech-magi were deeply respected by their peers.

During the Horus Heresy, one of the Deuterium Stars, Fusiria, turned traitor, while the other two, Magnax and Artos-Rho IV, were both overrun and destroyed. As a result of that threefold tragedy, Knights Preceptor became an increasingly rare commodity amongst the Noble houses, for their primary weapon could no longer be manufactured or maintained.

In M34, an Adeptus Mechanicus Explorator fleet scoured the Flensed Worlds for hidden knowledge and ancient archeotech. Supported by the Knights of House Krast, they successfully drove back the barbaric greenskins that had made the worlds their home, and liberated a great bounty for the Omnissiah. Amongst those riches was an STC for the las-impulsor, which was quickly – if respectfully – pressed into service. So it was that House Krast were honoured with the first new wave of Knights

Preceptor, and have possessed a disproportionately large number of them ever since. Gradually, replacement weapons and entire new chassis made their way out to numerous Knight worlds, and the Knights Preceptor became prevalent again.

It was in early M38 that a sizable force of Heretic Astartes descended upon the forge world of Ixas, where the holy las-impulsor STC was housed. Sweeping aside all resistance, the Chaos worshippers stole the device and bore it away into the Maelstrom. Thus was las-impulsor technology lost for a second time, and many corrupted Daemon Engines fashioned to torment the Imperium.

Yet this was not to be the end of the story. It was the Freeblade Moritor Repugnum that led a crusade force of Black Templars into the Maelstrom and tore the las-impulsor STC from the bloodied claws of the Dark Mechanicum. The machine was returned to Ixas with great ceremony in mid-M41, and has been in use ever since.

CANIS REX
THE CHAINBREAKER

When the Iron Warriors attacked the Knight world of Randoryn Alpha, the ruling House Cerberan marched out in force to deny them. The campaign was gruelling and merciless, the tides of battle flowing back and forth across the planet's rugged equatorial landmass. The Knights broke the Heretic Astartes' lines time and again, their magnificent charges shattering the Iron Warriors' strength and destroying their armoured siege trains. Yet one by one, the Knight suits fell or were crippled; one by one the strongholds of House Cerberan were besieged and laid low, and their serf chattel enslaved by the million.

After a final, courageous stand before the gates of the Stygian Keep, House Cerberan was defeated. The last of its Knight suits were disabled by invasive electrogheists, their pilots hauled out for torturous reconditioning.

Sir Hekhtur Cerberan was amongst those taken captive. The house's only surviving precept, the gruff old Noble did his best to inspire and bolster his comrades. Yet the horrors that the Iron Warriors inflicted were beyond imagining, and gradually they wore down the surviving Knights. As each warrior's spirit broke, so their Knight suits too were corrupted and transformed into heretical engines of destruction. Yet still Sir Hekhtur held out, chained within a dark oubliette, praying to the Emperor for deliverance.

Some say the Master of Mankind heard Hekhtur's prayers and sent him a miracle to reward his honour and faith. Others claim that Hekhtur's unusually strong bond with his Knight, Canis Rex, was the cause of the strange events that followed. Whatever the reason, all agree that Hekhtur was rescued from captivity by his Knight suit. Unpiloted, acting purely under the direction of its ferocious machine spirit, Canis Rex tore free of the Iron Warriors' remaking engines and blasted a path to its pilot with its las-impulsor. Freed from his chains, and with his captors in disarray, Sir Hekhtur was able to mount his Throne Mechanicum and – reunited with Canis Rex at last – make good his escape.

After taking the Freeblade oath as the last loyal Noble of his house, Sir Hekhtur led the Randorynian resistance, fighting back against the heretics wherever he could. He freed many enslaved serfs and managed to ferry them off-world to safety, earning his Freeblade epithet, Chainbreaker. Yet eventually even the grimly determined Hekhtur was forced to accept that his world was lost. Rather than throw his life away, Hekhtur took Canis Rex and the small complement of loyal Sacristans he had managed to save, stole an Imperial frigate, and set off to find a war that he could win for the Imperium. He has voyaged the stars ever since, freeing Imperial citizens enslaved by foul oppressors and punishing the scions of Chaos with vehemence and fury.

'The dark forces that assail Humanity will never cease their attack, and so neither shall I. The traitors, the heretics, the aliens – they began this fight, but we shall be the ones to finish it. The Emperor expects no less. Our enemies wield terror and cruelty as their weapons, thinking they can cow us into submission. I wield a crushing gauntlet and a damned enormous laser as mine, and I shall never submit. Were I a betting man, my lord, I know where I'd put my coin.'

- Sir Hekhtur the Chainbreaker, to Governor Doslyn before the Battle of Narsul Sound

KNIGHTS CASTELLAN

The Knight Castellan can be likened to a towering fortress, a bastion of Imperial might garrisoned by a single Noble lord and armed with an array of weapons so fearsome that they can tear the heart from an invading army. It is the foremost artillery platform within the lances of the knightly houses, hammering the enemy at extreme range from the moment the fight begins.

The Knight Castellan is one of the two most popular patterns of the Dominus-class chassis, the other being the Valiant. With its dual plasma core sending energy surging through its huge frame, the Castellan can mount a frightening array of weapons systems while maintaining its ion shield against incoming fire. Indeed, in extremis, Dominus pilots have even been known to overcharge their shield capacitors in order to temporarily project their shields over nearby allies to protect them from harm. It is considered both crass and unnecessary to do this for another Knight, but other Imperial forces fighting alongside Dominus Knights have been given good cause to thank the Nobles for their protection.

The arsenal of the Knight Castellan is legendary. On one arm they carry a plasma decimator, a huge and obliterative weapon capable of bathing swathes of the battlefield in searing energies and reducing the enemy to glowing ashes. Castellan pilots become adept at regulating the flow of plasmic energy from their dual cores to this potent weapon, even risking angering the machine spirits in order to unleash an especially ferocious blast should the situation demand it.

The Castellan's other armament is the volcano lance. Possessing massive range and stopping power, this laser cannon is the bane of super-heavy war engines and beasts. It can core out a lumbering Squiggoth or behead an enemy Titan, and when several Knights Castellan open fire at once, the effect is commensurate with the lance batteries of an Imperial Navy warship.

Upon the Castellan's broad shoulders are mounted twin siegebreaker cannons and shieldbreaker missile racks. The former are unsubtle gun turrets, fired by servitor-brain sub-arrays slaved to the pilot's targeting systems. They are capable of laying down a pounding bombardment of heavy ordnance to entirely carpet an area in flame and shrapnel. Shieldbreaker missiles, meanwhile, are an ancient variant of the redoubtable hunter-killer missile. These warheads incorporate raptoris machine spirits and empyric cascade micro-generators that allow them to disrupt and pass through enemy shields by skipping like hurled stones across the skin of reality, dipping minutely in and out of the warp in micro-second flickers. They are employed to punish those dishonourable enemies who cower behind veils of arcane energy or the massed ranks of lesser warriors. After all, as the pilots of the Knights Castellan are fond of saying, there is no escape from the Emperor's wrath.

KNIGHTS VALIANT

The Knight Valiant defeats its enemies through the simple principle of applying overwhelming firepower at close proximity. Marching relentlessly into the fight, gunfire scattering uselessly from its ion shield, the Valiant unleashes such devastating punishment against its targets in so short a space of time that they can neither fight back nor endure. Even a single Knight Valiant can break the back of an onrushing enemy horde, or shatter the centre of the foe's battle line like a battering ram smashing through a castle gate. When an entire lance of these fearsome war engines strides into battle, they can snap apart an enemy army like matchwood.

The Knight Valiant's primary armaments are its conflagration cannon and thundercoil harpoon. The former is a magnificently unsubtle weapon, comprising three enormous flamers linked together and fed from armoured promethium reservoirs. When triggered, the conflagration cannon spews forth an inescapable firestorm that washes over everything in range and reduces all to blackened ash. So does the Knight Valiant burn the Emperor's enemies as the worthless heretics they are.

The thundercoil harpoon is a rather more unusual weapon: a huge spear of adamantium fitted with pneumatic grapnels and attached by thick chains to an electrothaumic generator, allowing it to be fired then reeled back in time and again. Not only does its impaling mass gouge massive wounds in larger targets while crushing smaller victims outright, but once the harpoon has hit home, the Noble pilot can trigger their generator and send a massive electrical charge through the chain. Arcing electrogheists leap from the harpoon, cooking monstrous beasts from the inside and overloading the circuitry and power supplies of war engines.

Combined with the pummelling fire of its siegebreaker cannons and the inescapable detonations of its shieldbreaker missiles, it is not hard to see how many enemy forces soon disintegrate when the Valiant turns its wrath upon them. Those few who hold their ground often earn a salute of respect from the Knight Valiant's pilot before its next bombardment annihilates them utterly.

IN ADAMANT CLAD

Lances of Knights go to war in full and glorious panoply. Each towering engine proudly displays the colours and heraldry of house and Noble pilot both, making for a grand and fearsome martial spectacle.

Armiger Helverin of House Terryn with autocannons and heavy stubber

The full fury of House Terryn is unleashed upon the defences of the Black Legion. The ground shudders beneath the thunderous footfalls of the Knights and their Freeblade ally. The air fills with the howling and booming of their mighty weapons, and suddenly the barricades behind which the Heretic Astartes lurk seem a wholly inadequate form of defence.

The front face of the shoulder guard displays personal heraldry.

The volcano lance is a truly fearsome weapon of long-range death.

A Knight Castellan of House Terryn, Honour Absolute piloted by Lady Lorette. It is equipped with a volcano lance, plasma decimator, twin siegebreaker cannons and shieldbreaker missiles. This indomitable war engine displays the Imperial demi-aquila and horse head emblems of Terryn upon multiple armour plates.

This Noble's heraldry is an ivory background with two black stripes.

Many knightly weapons such as this reaper chainsword bear scrollwork titles on their housings.

A Knight Errant of House Terryn, Vermilion Shield piloted by Baron Capulan. It is equipped with a thermal cannon and reaper chainsword. The pennant that hangs between the Knight's legs evidences an array of honour kills claimed by its pilot, while its tilting shield is decorated with the full crest of House Terryn in all its glory.

The towering Knights of House Terryn march into battle alongside the ferocious warriors of the Blood Angels Death Company. Between the fire and fury of the Knights' guns, and the point-blank ferocity of Sanguinius' sons, the streets of the Imperial city will soon be scoured of enemies.

Tilting shield honour markings and purity seal

The avenger gatling cannon boasts a ferocious rate of fire and armour-busting ammunition to mow down infantry and light vehicles alike.

A Knight Crusader of House Taranis, Red Might piloted by Sir Drantar. It is equipped with a battle cannon, avenger gatling cannon and a twin Icarus autocannon. The crest of House Taranis is displayed on this Knight's tilting shield, while honour markings earned by its pilot can be seen on the pennant that hangs between the Knight's legs.

Many Questor Mechanicus Knights display sacred industrial chevrons on their weaponry and hulls.

The white band on this battle cannon is used to denote battlefield veterancy earned through multiple super-heavy kills.

A Knight Paladin of House Raven, Unyielding Iron piloted by Sir Walkorn. The sacred chevron design shown upon the Knight's reaper chainsword mark its pilot out as a veteran warrior, greatly honoured by their peers. Meanwhile, the icon of House Raven is clearly displayed upon the front facings of the Knight's shoulder guards and shin plating.

Much of the thundercoil harpoon's casing is taken up by a huge winch-coil and electro-generatorum.

A Knight Valiant of House Raven, Divine Retribution piloted by Sir Galen. It is equipped with shieldbreaker missiles and a twin siegebreaker cannon. The Mechanicus cog indicates House Raven's proud allegiance to the Adeptus Mechanicus of Mars.

Armiger Warglaive thermal spear, shown above, and reaper chain-cleaver, shown below

Left: Armiger Warglaive of House Raven with thermal spear, reaper chain-cleaver and carapace-mounted meltagun

Right: The carapace of this House Raven Armiger Warglaive is mounted with a heavy stubber.

The Knights of House Raven advance into battle alongside the armoured transports of the Cadian Astra Militarum. Like mobile fortresses bristling with massive guns, the Knights loom over their allies and promise death to their enemies.

Former High King Neru Degallio pilots the Freeblade known as the White Warden. Here, he advances through the blasted barricades of a ruined city on Dekhorra VI, ready to hammer the Ork invaders with his rapid-fire battle cannon.

Gerantius' ancient reaper chainsword is a potent weapon, its housing edged with weathered copper and brass.

Gerantius' shoulder guard displays his heraldry as gatekeeper of Alaric Prime.

This Freeblade Knight Errant bearing a thermal cannon and reaper chainsword is Gerantius, often called the Forgotten Knight. The significance of his ancient heraldry is lost to modern comprehension, but it has been the last sight of many of the Imperium's foes.

Every element of the Obsidian Knight's heraldry is macabre, from the repeated red-eyed skull motif to the near-blasphemy of the skeletal aquila.

This death's head design is the Obsidian Knight's personal sigil.

The sable armour plates and morbid iconography of this Knight Paladin reveal it to be the much-feared Obsidian Knight. Equipped with a rapid-fire battle cannon and reaper chainsword, this mysterious Freeblade has fought in many battles on the Eastern Fringe.

Amidst the arc-lit glare of a night-time offensive upon Gudrun, the Freeblade known as Amaranthine stands fast to anchor the Imperial battle line. Neither heretic, traitor nor mutant shall pass…

Canis Rex bears a vast wealth of
battle honours.

Sir Hekhtur enthroned within his raised
pilot's compartment

Sir Hekhtur, dismounted and clad in his
half-armoured bodyglove

Canis Rex,
the Chainbreaker

GODS OF WAR

An Imperial Knights army comprises a collection of towering war engines, even the smallest of which looms over its enemies like an adamantine giant. There are countless ways to assemble such a force, but most armies will typically begin with a handful of Knights, a core from which a larger force can develop.

Everyone has their own preferred method of collecting a Warhammer 40,000 army. Many people are inspired by the models themselves; others are driven by considerations of how the army will perform on the battlefield, painting or modelling projects they are motivated by, or a stirring narrative they wish to evoke with their models.

The example army below is comprised of one of every class of Imperial Knight

– the Armiger, the Questoris and the Dominus. It provides a great starting point for a larger collection, and opportunities to build, paint and play with a variety of models.

The force is led by Lord Grevan of House Raven, a renowned Princeps devoted to the Omnissiah and enthroned within the Knight Warden known as Ferrous Maximus. Providing his allies overwhelming firepower is Sir Galen,

who pilots a Knight Valiant named Divine Retribution. Meanwhile, the force gains additional close-range punch through its Armiger Warglaive, Venator Vulkis, piloted by Sir Terreven. Comprising three Lords of War, this force not only provides an excellent start to an Imperial Knights army, but also fulfils the requirements of a Battle-forged Super-heavy Detachment, meaning that it goes to battle with an impressive six Command Points to spend on Stratagems.

The Knights of Lord Grevan's House Raven lance bring the fight to the enemies of the Omnissiah.

HIGH KING TYBALT'S CRUSADING HOST

Many Imperial Knight collections begin with a single – albeit impressive – model, but they can swiftly grow into a host of mighty war engines such as the one pictured here.

This army represents a knightly host belonging to the Imperial-aligned House Terryn. Comprising a range of different classes and patterns of Imperial Knights, it is a force capable of facing any enemy on the field of battle and holding its own, while also presenting an exciting and varied range of painting and modelling opportunities for the collector.

The army is led by none other than High King Tybalt of House Terryn, who pilots the redoubtable Knight Warden known as Fury of Voltoris. Tybalt is the army's Warlord, making him the heroic lynchpin of the entire force. Moreover, his Knight Warden offers an exceptional balance of heavy firepower and

close-quarters prowess that makes Tybalt the equal of any of the enemy's champions.

Tybalt leads a lance of two other Knights. The first of these is Sir Opheron, who pilots a Knight Paladin named Unyielding Victory. This venerable war engine is an excellent all-rounder, able to support King Tybalt in laying down ranged bombardments or carving the enemy up in close combat as needed. The lance is completed by Honour Absolute, a hulking Knight Castellan piloted by the renowned Lady Lorette. Equipped with a veritable arsenal of heavy long-ranged weaponry, Honour Absolute can annihilate the foe from a distance or end enemy attacks before they even begin.

The army's second lance is led by Baron Capulan, who pilots the Knight Errant known as Vermilion Shield. He is amongst the most aggressively tempered Nobles of House Terryn, and his Knight's armaments are well suited to driving headlong into the foe. He is flanked by Sir Kosker, in the Warglaive Bellicose Huntsman, and Lady Tabithorne, who pilots the Warglaive Sword of Truth. This trio forms a hard-hitting close-assault spearhead to shatter the enemy lines.

The army is completed by the inclusion of the famed Freeblade Canis Rex. This Knight Preceptor's potent weapons allow it to devastate the enemy at close to medium range, making it an excellent asset to support its Terryn comrades on the field of battle.

This army fulfils the requirements of two Super-heavy Detachments. As it is also Battle-forged, its player receives nine Command Points to spend on Stratagems such as Full Tilt, which allows a Knight to quickly cross the battlefield and get to grips with the foe.

1. High King Tybalt piloting the Knight Warden Fury of Voltoris

2. Sir Opheron piloting the Knight Paladin Unyielding Victory

3. Lady Lorette piloting the Knight Castellan Honour Absolute

4. Baron Capulan piloting the Knight Errant Vermilion Shield

5. Sir Kosker piloting the Armiger Warglaive Bellicose Huntsman

6. Lady Tabithorne piloting the Armiger Warglaive Sword of Truth

7. Sir Hekhtur piloting the Freeblade Knight Preceptor Canis Rex

KNIGHTLY HOST

This section contains all of the datasheets that you will need to fight battles with your Imperial Knights miniatures, and the rules for all of the weapons they can wield in battle. Each datasheet includes the characteristics profiles of the unit it describes, as well as any wargear and special abilities it may have.

KEYWORDS

Throughout this section you will come across keywords that are within angular brackets, specifically <Questor Allegiance> and <Household>. These are shorthand for keywords of your own choosing, as described below.

<Questor Allegiance>

All Imperial Knights owe allegiance to either the Imperium of Man or the Machine Cult of the Adeptus Mechanicus. Even Freeblades, who no longer belong to a Noble house, maintain the oath of allegiance they swore long ago.

Imperial Knights datasheets have the <Questor Allegiance> keyword. When you include such a unit in your army, you must nominate whether that unit owes its allegiance to the Imperium or the Adeptus Mechanicus. If the former, then you replace the <Questor Allegiance> keyword in every instance on that unit's datasheet with Questor Imperialis; if the latter, you replace the <Questor Allegiance> keyword in every instance on that unit's datasheet with Questor Mechanicus.

For example, if you were to include a Knight Preceptor in your army, and you decided it owed allegiance to the Adeptus Mechanicus, its <Questor Allegiance> keyword is changed to Questor Mechanicus.

<Household>

With the exception of Freeblades, all Imperial Knights belong to a Noble household.

Imperial Knights datasheets have the <Household> keyword. When you include such a unit in your army, you must nominate which household that unit is from (unless it is a Freeblade, as described opposite). You then simply replace the <Household> keyword in every instance on that unit's datasheet with the name of your chosen household. If the unit has the Questor Imperialis keyword, it must come from a household that owes allegiance to the Imperium; if the unit has the Questor Mechanicus keyword, it must come from a household that owes allegiance to the Adeptus Mechanicus. You can use any of the Noble households that you have read about, or you can make up your own.

For example, if you were to include a Knight Preceptor in your army that has the Questor Mechanicus keyword, you could then decide it was from House Raven. Its <Household> keyword is then changed to House Raven, and its 'Mentor' ability would say 'Re-roll hit rolls of 1 for friendly House Raven Armiger Class units within 6" of this model.'

You can instead nominate any Imperial Knight to be a Freeblade, regardless of whether it owes allegiance to the Imperium or the Adeptus Mechanicus. If you do so, replace the <Household> keyword in every instance on that unit's datasheet with the Freeblade keyword.

'I have fought across a score of worlds in the Emperor's name. I have slaughtered traitors, xenos and heretics for the honour of my house. I have known glorious victory… and painful defeat. Yet I shall never tire, never cease and never relent, for ours is a duty that will never end.'

- Lady Karina Griffith

IMPERIAL KNIGHTS WARGEAR LIST

Many of the units you will find on the following pages reference the *Carapace Weapons* list. When this is the case, the unit may take any item from the list below. The profiles for the weapons in this list can be found in the Knightly Armaments section (pg 102-103).

CARAPACE WEAPONS

- Ironstorm missile pod
- Stormspear rocket pod
- Twin Icarus autocannon

ARMIGER HELVERIN

NAME	M	WS	BS	S	T	W	A	Ld	Sv
Armiger Helverin	*	*	*	6	7	12	4	8	3+

DAMAGE
Some of this model's characteristics change as it suffers damage, as shown below:

REMAINING W	M	WS	BS
7-12+	14"	3+	3+
4-6	10"	4+	4+
1-3	7"	5+	5+

This unit contains 1 Armiger Helverin. It can include 1 additional Armiger Helverin (**Power Level +9**), or 2 additional Armiger Helverins (**Power Level +18**). Each Armiger Helverin is equipped with two Armiger autocannons and a heavy stubber.

WEAPON	RANGE	TYPE	S	AP	D	ABILITIES
Armiger autocannon	60"	Heavy 2D3	7	-1	3	Ignore the penalty to hit rolls for moving and firing this Heavy weapon.
Heavy stubber	36"	Heavy 3	4	0	1	-
Meltagun	12"	Assault 1	8	-4	D6	If the target is within half range of this weapon, roll two dice when inflicting damage with it and discard the lowest result.

WARGEAR OPTIONS
• Any model may replace its heavy stubber with a meltagun.

ABILITIES
Ion Shield: Models in this unit have a 5+ invulnerable save against ranged weapons. **Explodes:** Each time a model in this unit is reduced to 0 wounds, roll a dice before removing it from the battlefield; on a 6 it explodes, and each unit within 6" suffers D3 mortal wounds.	**Vehicle Squadron:** The first time this unit is set up, all of its models must be placed within 6" of each other. From that point onwards, each operates independently and is treated as a separate unit.

FACTION KEYWORDS	IMPERIUM, IMPERIAL KNIGHTS, <QUESTOR ALLEGIANCE>, <HOUSEHOLD>
KEYWORDS	VEHICLE, ARMIGER CLASS, ARMIGER HELVERIN

ARMIGER WARGLAIVE

NAME	M	WS	BS	S	T	W	A	Ld	Sv
Armiger Warglaive	*	*	*	6	7	12	4	8	3+

DAMAGE
Some of this model's characteristics change as it suffers damage, as shown below:

REMAINING W	M	WS	BS
7-12+	14"	3+	3+
4-6	10"	4+	4+
1-3	7"	5+	5+

This unit contains 1 Armiger Warglaive. It can include 1 additional Armiger Warglaive (**Power Level +9**), or 2 additional Armiger Warglaives (**Power Level +18**). Each Armiger Warglaive is equipped with a reaper chain-cleaver, thermal spear and heavy stubber.

WEAPON	RANGE	TYPE	S	AP	D	ABILITIES
Heavy stubber	36"	Heavy 3	4	0	1	-
Meltagun	12"	Assault 1	8	-4	D6	If the target is within half range of this weapon, roll two dice when inflicting damage with it and discard the lowest result.
Thermal spear	30"	Assault D3	8	-4	D6	If the target is within half range of this weapon, roll two dice when inflicting damage with it and discard the lowest result.
Reaper chain-cleaver	When attacking with this weapon, choose one of the profiles below:					
- Strike	Melee	Melee	x2	-3	3	-
- Sweep	Melee	Melee	User	-2	1	Make 2 hit rolls for each attack made with this weapon, instead of 1.

WARGEAR OPTIONS
• Any model may replace its heavy stubber with a meltagun.

ABILITIES
Ion Shield: Models in this unit have a 5+ invulnerable save against ranged weapons. **Explodes:** Each time a model in this unit is reduced to 0 wounds, roll a dice before removing it from the battlefield; on a 6 it explodes, and each unit within 6" suffers D3 mortal wounds.	**Vehicle Squadron:** The first time this unit is set up, all of its models must be placed within 6" of each other. From that point onwards, each operates independently and is treated as a separate unit.

FACTION KEYWORDS	IMPERIUM, IMPERIAL KNIGHTS, <QUESTOR ALLEGIANCE>, <HOUSEHOLD>
KEYWORDS	VEHICLE, ARMIGER CLASS, ARMIGER WARGLAIVE

KNIGHT PRECEPTOR

DAMAGE			
Some of this model's characteristics change as it suffers damage, as shown below:			
REMAINING W	M	WS	BS
13-24+	12"	3+	3+
7-12	9"	4+	4+
1-6	6"	5+	5+

NAME	M	WS	BS	S	T	W	A	Ld	Sv
Knight Preceptor	*	*	*	8	8	24	4	9	3+

A Knight Preceptor is a single model equipped with a reaper chainsword, las-impulsor, heavy stubber and titanic feet.

WEAPON	RANGE	TYPE	S	AP	D	ABILITIES
Heavy stubber	36"	Heavy 3	4	0	1	-
Las-impulsor	When attacking with this weapon, choose one of the profiles below.					
- Low intensity	36"	Heavy 2D6	6	-2	D3	-
- High intensity	18"	Heavy D6	12	-4	D6	-.
Meltagun	12"	Assault 1	8	-4	D6	If the target is within half range of this weapon, roll two dice when inflicting damage with it and discard the lowest result.
Multi-laser	36"	Heavy 3	6	0	1	-
Reaper chainsword	Melee	Melee	+6	-3	6	-
Thunderstrike gauntlet	Melee	Melee	x2	-4	6	When attacking with this weapon, you must subtract 1 from the hit roll. If a VEHICLE or MONSTER is slain by this weapon, pick an enemy unit within 9" of the bearer and roll a D6. On a 4+ that unit suffers D3 mortal wounds.
Titanic feet	Melee	Melee	User	-2	D3	Make 3 hit rolls for each attack made with this weapon.

WARGEAR OPTIONS	
	• This model may take an item from the *Carapace Weapons* list. • This model may replace its reaper chainsword with a thunderstrike gauntlet. • This model may replace its heavy stubber with a meltagun or multi-laser.

ABILITIES	
	Ion Shield: This model has a 5+ invulnerable save against ranged weapons. **Explodes:** If this model is reduced to 0 wounds, roll a D6 before removing it from the battlefield. On a 6 it explodes, and each unit within 2D6" suffers D6 mortal wounds. **Mentor:** Re-roll hit rolls of 1 for friendly <HOUSEHOLD> ARMIGER CLASS units within 6" of this model.	**Super-heavy Walker:** This model can Fall Back in the Movement phase and still shoot and/or charge in the same turn. When this model Falls Back, it can move over enemy INFANTRY and SWARM models, though it must end its move more than 1" from any enemy units. In addition, this model can move and fire Heavy weapons without suffering the penalty to its hit rolls. Finally, this model only gains a bonus to its save for being in cover if at least half of the model is obscured from the firer.

FACTION KEYWORDS	IMPERIUM, IMPERIAL KNIGHTS, <QUESTOR ALLEGIANCE>, <HOUSEHOLD>
KEYWORDS	TITANIC, VEHICLE, QUESTORIS CLASS, KNIGHT PRECEPTOR

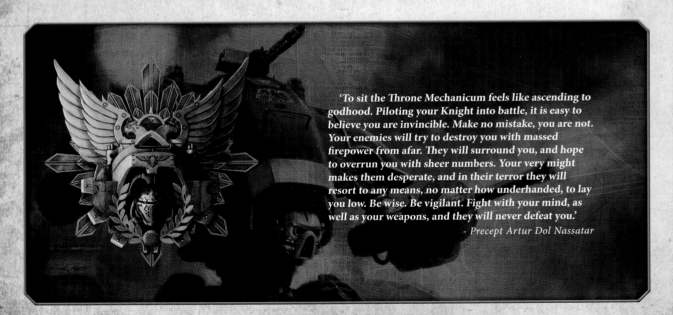

'To sit the Throne Mechanicum feels like ascending to godhood. Piloting your Knight into battle, it is easy to believe you are invincible. Make no mistake, you are not. Your enemies will try to destroy you with massed firepower from afar. They will surround you, and hope to overrun you with sheer numbers. Your very might makes them desperate, and in their terror they will resort to any means, no matter how underhanded, to lay you low. Be wise. Be vigilant. Fight with your mind, as well as your weapons, and they will never defeat you.'

- Precept Artur Dol Nassatar

KNIGHT PALADIN

NAME	M	WS	BS	S	T	W	A	Ld	Sv
Knight Paladin	*	*	*	8	8	24	4	9	3+

DAMAGE

Some of this model's characteristics change as it suffers damage, as shown below:

REMAINING W	M	WS	BS
13-24+	12"	3+	3+
7-12	9"	4+	4+
1-6	6"	5+	5+

A Knight Paladin is a single model equipped with a reaper chainsword, rapid-fire battle cannon, two heavy stubbers and titanic feet.

WEAPON	RANGE	TYPE	S	AP	D	ABILITIES
Heavy stubber	36"	Heavy 3	4	0	1	-
Meltagun	12"	Assault 1	8	-4	D6	If the target is within half range of this weapon, roll two dice when inflicting damage with it and discard the lowest result.
Rapid-fire battle cannon	72"	Heavy 2D6	8	-2	D3	-
Reaper chainsword	Melee	Melee	+6	-3	6	-
Thunderstrike gauntlet	Melee	Melee	x2	-4	6	When attacking with this weapon, you must subtract 1 from the hit roll. If a **VEHICLE** or **MONSTER** is slain by this weapon, pick an enemy unit within 9" of the bearer and roll a D6. On a 4+ that unit suffers D3 mortal wounds.
Titanic feet	Melee	Melee	User	-2	D3	Make 3 hit rolls for each attack made with this weapon.

WARGEAR OPTIONS	• This model may take an item from the *Carapace Weapons* list. • This model may replace its reaper chainsword with a thunderstrike gauntlet. • This model may replace one heavy stubber with a meltagun.

ABILITIES

Ion Shield: This model has a 5+ invulnerable save against ranged weapons.

Explodes: If this model is reduced to 0 wounds, roll a D6 before removing it from the battlefield. On a 6 it explodes, and each unit within 2D6" suffers D6 mortal wounds.

Super-heavy Walker: This model can Fall Back in the Movement phase and still shoot and/or charge in the same turn. When this model Falls Back, it can move over enemy **INFANTRY** and **SWARM** models, though it must end its move more than 1" from any enemy units. In addition, this model can move and fire Heavy weapons without suffering the penalty to its hit rolls. Finally, this model only gains a bonus to its save for being in cover if at least half of the model is obscured from the firer.

FACTION KEYWORDS	IMPERIUM, IMPERIAL KNIGHTS, \<QUESTOR ALLEGIANCE\>, \<HOUSEHOLD\>
KEYWORDS	TITANIC, VEHICLE, QUESTORIS CLASS, KNIGHT PALADIN

A Knight Paladin of House Terryn advances through the ruins of an Imperial hive city.

22 POWER

KNIGHT ERRANT

NAME	M	WS	BS	S	T	W	A	Ld	Sv
Knight Errant	*	*	*	8	8	24	4	9	3+

A Knight Errant is a single model equipped with a reaper chainsword, thermal cannon, heavy stubber and titanic feet.

DAMAGE

Some of this model's characteristics change as it suffers damage, as shown below:

REMAINING W	M	WS	BS
13-24+	12"	3+	3+
7-12	9"	4+	4+
1-6	6"	5+	5+

WEAPON	RANGE	TYPE	S	AP	D	ABILITIES
Heavy stubber	36"	Heavy 3	4	0	1	-
Meltagun	12"	Assault 1	8	-4	D6	If the target is within half range of this weapon, roll two dice when inflicting damage with it and discard the lowest result.
Thermal cannon	36"	Heavy D6	9	-4	D6	If the target is within half range of this weapon, roll two dice when inflicting damage with it and discard the lowest result.
Reaper chainsword	Melee	Melee	+6	-3	6	-
Thunderstrike gauntlet	Melee	Melee	x2	-4	6	When attacking with this weapon, you must subtract 1 from the hit roll. If a **Vehicle** or **Monster** is slain by this weapon, pick an enemy unit within 9" of the bearer and roll a D6. On a 4+ that unit suffers D3 mortal wounds.
Titanic feet	Melee	Melee	User	-2	D3	Make 3 hit rolls for each attack made with this weapon.

WARGEAR OPTIONS	• This model may take an item from the *Carapace Weapons* list. • This model may replace its reaper chainsword with a thunderstrike gauntlet. • This model may replace its heavy stubber with a meltagun.

ABILITIES	**Ion Shield:** This model has a 5+ invulnerable save against ranged weapons. **Explodes:** If this model is reduced to 0 wounds, roll a D6 before removing it from the battlefield. On a 6 it explodes, and each unit within 2D6" suffers D6 mortal wounds.	**Super-heavy Walker:** This model can Fall Back in the Movement phase and still shoot and/or charge in the same turn. When this model Falls Back it can move over enemy **Infantry** and **Swarm** models, though it must end its move more than 1" from any enemy units. In addition, this model can move and fire Heavy weapons without suffering the penalty to its hit rolls. Finally, this model only gains a bonus to its save for being in cover if at least half of the model is obscured from the firer.

FACTION KEYWORDS	**Imperium, Imperial Knights, <Questor Allegiance>, <Household>**

KEYWORDS	**Titanic, Vehicle, Questoris Class, Knight Errant**

'The Errant is surely the finest of Knights. A cannon of unsurpassed power, against which no heretic armour is proof. A blade fit to cut down the most monstrous beasts in honourable close-quarters combat. A fiery warrior spirit the equal of even the most bellicose pilot. Yes, give me a Knight Errant, and I shall deliver you victory.'

- Sir Tadwynne of House Boros

94

KNIGHT GALLANT

NAME	M	WS	BS	S	T	W	A	Ld	Sv
Knight Gallant	*	*	*	8	8	24	5	9	3+

DAMAGE

Some of this model's characteristics change as it suffers damage, as shown below:

REMAINING W	M	WS	BS
13-24+	12"	2+	3+
7-12	9"	3+	4+
1-6	6"	4+	5+

A Knight Gallant is a single model equipped with a reaper chainsword, thunderstrike gauntlet, heavy stubber and titanic feet.

WEAPON	RANGE	TYPE	S	AP	D	ABILITIES
Heavy stubber	36"	Heavy 3	4	0	1	-
Meltagun	12"	Assault 1	8	-4	D6	If the target is within half range of this weapon, roll two dice when inflicting damage with it and discard the lowest result.
Reaper chainsword	Melee	Melee	+6	-3	6	-
Thunderstrike gauntlet	Melee	Melee	x2	-4	6	When attacking with this weapon, you must subtract 1 from the hit roll. If a **VEHICLE** or **MONSTER** is slain by this weapon, pick an enemy unit within 9" of the bearer and roll a D6. On a 4+ that unit suffers D3 mortal wounds.
Titanic feet	Melee	Melee	User	-2	D3	Make 3 hit rolls for each attack made with this weapon.

WARGEAR OPTIONS	• This model may take an item from the *Carapace Weapons* list. • This model may replace its heavy stubber with a meltagun.

ABILITIES	**Ion Shield:** This model has a 5+ invulnerable save against ranged weapons. **Explodes:** If this model is reduced to 0 wounds, roll a D6 before removing it from the battlefield. On a 6 it explodes, and each unit within 2D6" suffers D6 mortal wounds.	**Super-heavy Walker:** This model can Fall Back in the Movement phase and still shoot and/or charge in the same turn. When this model Falls Back it can move over enemy **INFANTRY** and **SWARM** models, though it must end its move more than 1" from any enemy units. In addition, this model can move and fire Heavy weapons without suffering the penalty to its hit rolls. Finally, this model only gains a bonus to its save for being in cover if at least half of the model is obscured from the firer.

FACTION KEYWORDS	IMPERIUM, IMPERIAL KNIGHTS, <QUESTOR ALLEGIANCE>, <HOUSEHOLD>

KEYWORDS	TITANIC, VEHICLE, QUESTORIS CLASS, KNIGHT GALLANT

Knights of House Raven advance into battle alongside the warriors of the Ultramarines Chapter.

Ever vigilant, a Knight Warden of House Cadmus defends an Imperial cathedrum.

KNIGHT WARDEN

23 POWER

NAME	M	WS	BS	S	T	W	A	Ld	Sv
Knight Warden	*	*	*	8	8	24	4	9	3+

A Knight Warden is a single model equipped with a reaper chainsword, avenger gatling cannon, heavy stubber, heavy flamer and titanic feet.

DAMAGE
Some of this model's characteristics change as it suffers damage, as shown below:

REMAINING W	M	WS	BS
13-24+	12"	3+	3+
7-12	9"	4+	4+
1-6	6"	5+	5+

WEAPON	RANGE	TYPE	S	AP	D	ABILITIES
Avenger gatling cannon	36"	Heavy 12	6	-2	2	-
Heavy flamer	8"	Heavy D6	5	-1	1	This weapon automatically hits its target.
Heavy stubber	36"	Heavy 3	4	0	1	-
Meltagun	12"	Assault 1	8	-4	D6	If the target is within half range of this weapon, roll two dice when inflicting damage with it and discard the lowest result.
Reaper chainsword	Melee	Melee	+6	-3	6	
Thunderstrike gauntlet	Melee	Melee	x2	-4	6	When attacking with this weapon, you must subtract 1 from the hit roll. If a VEHICLE or MONSTER is slain by this weapon, pick an enemy unit within 9" of the bearer and roll a D6. On a 4+ that unit suffers D3 mortal wounds.
Titanic feet	Melee	Melee	User	-2	D3	Make 3 hit rolls for each attack made with this weapon.

WARGEAR OPTIONS	• This model may take an item from the *Carapace Weapons* list. • This model may replace its reaper chainsword with a thunderstrike gauntlet. • This model may replace its heavy stubber with a meltagun.

ABILITIES	**Ion Shield:** This model has a 5+ invulnerable save against ranged weapons. **Explodes:** If this model is reduced to 0 wounds, roll a D6 before removing it from the battlefield. On a 6 it explodes, and each unit within 2D6" suffers D6 mortal wounds.	**Super-heavy Walker:** This model can Fall Back in the Movement phase and still shoot and/or charge in the same turn. When this model Falls Back it can move over enemy **INFANTRY** and **SWARM** models, though it must end its move more than 1" from any enemy units. In addition, this model can move and fire Heavy weapons without suffering the penalty to its hit rolls. Finally, this model only gains a bonus to its save for being in cover if at least half of the model is obscured from the firer.

FACTION KEYWORDS	IMPERIUM, IMPERIAL KNIGHTS, <QUESTOR ALLEGIANCE>, <HOUSEHOLD>
KEYWORDS	TITANIC, VEHICLE, QUESTORIS CLASS, KNIGHT WARDEN

KNIGHT CRUSADER

DAMAGE

Some of this model's characteristics change as it suffers damage, as shown below:

REMAINING W	M	WS	BS
13-24+	12"	3+	3+
7-12	9"	4+	4+
1-6	6"	5+	5+

NAME	M	WS	BS	S	T	W	A	Ld	Sv
Knight Crusader	✳	✳	✳	8	8	24	4	9	3+

A Knight Crusader is a single model equipped with a thermal cannon, avenger gatling cannon, heavy stubber, heavy flamer and titanic feet.

WEAPON	RANGE	TYPE	S	AP	D	ABILITIES
Avenger gatling cannon	36"	Heavy 12	6	-2	2	-
Heavy flamer	8"	Heavy D6	5	-1	1	This weapon automatically hits its target.
Heavy stubber	36"	Heavy 3	4	0	1	-
Meltagun	12"	Assault 1	8	-4	D6	If the target is within half range of this weapon, roll two dice when inflicting damage with it and discard the lowest result.
Rapid-fire battle cannon	72"	Heavy 2D6	8	-2	D3	-
Thermal cannon	36"	Heavy D6	9	-4	D6	If the target is within half range of this weapon, roll two dice when inflicting damage with it and discard the lowest result.
Titanic feet	Melee	Melee	User	-2	D3	Make 3 hit rolls for each attack made with this weapon.

WARGEAR OPTIONS	• This model may take an item from the *Carapace Weapons* list. • This model may replace its thermal cannon with a rapid-fire battle cannon and a heavy stubber. • This model may replace one heavy stubber with a meltagun.

ABILITIES	**Ion Shield:** This model has a 5+ invulnerable save against ranged weapons. **Explodes:** If this model is reduced to 0 wounds, roll a D6 before removing it from the battlefield. On a 6 it explodes, and each unit within 2D6" suffers D6 mortal wounds.	**Super-heavy Walker:** This model can Fall Back in the Movement phase and still shoot and/or charge in the same turn. When this model Falls Back, it can move over enemy **INFANTRY** and **SWARM** models, though it must end its move more than 1" from any enemy units. In addition, this model can move and fire Heavy weapons without suffering the penalty to its hit rolls. Finally, this model only gains a bonus to its save for being in cover if at least half of the model is obscured from the firer.

FACTION KEYWORDS	IMPERIUM, IMPERIAL KNIGHTS, <QUESTOR ALLEGIANCE>, <HOUSEHOLD>

KEYWORDS	TITANIC, VEHICLE, QUESTORIS CLASS, KNIGHT CRUSADER

A Knight Crusader of House Taranis looms over the devastation wrought by its own fearsome firepower.

CANIS REX

NAME	M	WS	BS	S	T	W	A	Ld	Sv
Canis Rex	*	*	*	8	8	24	4	9	3+
Sir Hekhtur	6"	3+	3+	3	3	4	3	9	4+

DAMAGE
Some of Canis Rex's characteristics change as it suffers damage, as shown below:

REMAINING W	M	WS	BS
13-24+	12"	2+	2+
7-12	9"	3+	3+
1-6	6"	4+	4+

Canis Rex is a single model equipped with a las-impulsor, multi-laser, Freedom's Hand and titanic feet.
Sir Hekhtur begins the battle piloting Canis Rex (see the Sir Hekhtur ability below). Only one of this unit may be included in your army.

WEAPON	RANGE	TYPE	S	AP	D	ABILITIES
Archeotech pistol	15"	Pistol 1	5	-2	2	-
Las-impulsor	When attacking with this weapon, choose one of the profiles below.					
- Low intensity	36"	Heavy 2D6	6	-2	D3	-
- High intensity	18"	Heavy D6	12	-4	D6	-
Multi-laser	36"	Heavy 3	6	0	1	-
Freedom's Hand	Melee	Melee	x2	-4	2D6	When attacking with this weapon, you must subtract 1 from the hit roll. Treat any damage roll less than 6 made with this weapon as 6 instead. If a VEHICLE or MONSTER is slain by this weapon, pick an enemy unit within 9" of the bearer and roll a D6. On a 4+ that unit suffers D3 mortal wounds.
Titanic feet	Melee	Melee	User	-2	D3	Make 3 hit rolls for each attack made with this weapon.

ABILITIES

Ion Shield: CANIS REX has a 5+ invulnerable save against ranged weapons.

Explodes: If CANIS REX is reduced to 0 wounds, roll a D6 before removing it from the battlefield. On a 6 it explodes, and each unit within 2D6" suffers D6 mortal wounds.

Sir Hekhtur: If CANIS REX is reduced to 0 wounds but does not explode, set up Sir Hekhtur within 3" of it before CANIS REX is removed. He is treated as a passenger disembarking from a destroyed transport. Assuming he survives, Sir Hekhtur then uses his own profile above and his own keywords below, and is armed with an archeotech pistol. This unit is not considered to have been destroyed until Sir Hekhtur is slain.

Chainbreaker: Roll a D6 each time a friendly IMPERIUM model flees whilst within 6" of CANIS REX; on a 6 that model does not flee.

Super-heavy Walker: CANIS REX can Fall Back in the Movement phase and still shoot and/or charge in the same turn. When CANIS REX Falls Back, it can move over enemy INFANTRY and SWARM models, though it must end its move more than 1" from any enemy units. In addition, CANIS REX can move and fire Heavy weapons without suffering the penalty to its hit rolls. Finally, CANIS REX only gains a bonus to its save for being in cover if at least half of the model is obscured from the firer.

FACTION KEYWORDS	IMPERIUM, IMPERIAL KNIGHTS, QUESTOR IMPERIALIS, FREEBLADE
KEYWORDS (CANIS REX)	CHARACTER, TITANIC, VEHICLE, QUESTORIS CLASS, KNIGHT PRECEPTOR, CANIS REX
KEYWORDS (SIR HEKHTUR)	CHARACTER, INFANTRY, SIR HEKHTUR

'There are none so detestable in all the length and breadth of the Imperium as those who make slaves of its loyal servants. Honest toil in the Emperor's name is one thing, for through industrious labour and needful hardship does a man ready his soul to receive the Emperor's grace. But when the alien or the heretic places the yoke of slavery upon the necks of honest Imperial citizens, and turns their good works to foul ends, that is a sin of unforgivable magnitude. There is only one punishment fitting for such abominable tyrants… Death.'
- Sir Hekhtur, the Chainbreaker

KNIGHT CASTELLAN

NAME	M	WS	BS	S	T	W	A	Ld	Sv
Knight Castellan	*	*	*	8	8	28	4	9	3+

A Knight Castellan is a single model equipped with a plasma decimator, volcano lance, two shieldbreaker missiles, two twin meltaguns, two twin siegebreaker cannons and titanic feet.

DAMAGE

Some of this model's characteristics change as it suffers damage, as shown below:

REMAINING W	M	WS	BS
15-28+	10"	4+	3+
8-14	7"	5+	4+
1-7	4"	6+	5+

WEAPON	RANGE	TYPE	S	AP	D	ABILITIES
Plasma decimator	When attacking with this weapon, choose one of the profiles below.					
- Standard	48"	Heavy 2D6	7	-3	1	-
- Supercharge	48"	Heavy 2D6	8	-3	2	For each hit roll of 1, the bearer suffers 1 mortal wound after all of this weapon's shots have been resolved.
Shieldbreaker missile	48"	Heavy 1	10	-4	D6	Each shieldbreaker missile can only be fired once per battle, and a model can only fire one each turn. Invulnerable saving throws cannot be made against wounds caused by this weapon.
Twin siegebreaker cannon	48"	Heavy 2D3	7	-1	D3	
Twin meltagun	12"	Assault 2	8	-4	D6	If the target is within half range of this weapon, roll two dice when inflicting damage with it and discard the lowest result.
Volcano lance	80"	Heavy D6	14	-5	3D3	You can re-roll failed wound rolls when targeting **TITANIC** units with this weapon.
Titanic feet	Melee	Melee	User	-2	D3	Make 3 hit rolls for each attack made with this weapon.

WARGEAR OPTIONS	• This model may replace one of its twin siegebreaker cannons with two shieldbreaker missiles.

ABILITIES	**Ion Shield:** This model has a 5+ invulnerable save against ranged weapons. **Dual Plasma Core Explosion:** If this model is reduced to 0 wounds, roll 2D6 before removing it from the battlefield. If you roll a 6 on either dice, it explodes, and each unit within 2D6" suffers D6 mortal wounds; if you roll a 6 on both dice, each unit within 3D6" suffers D6 mortal wounds instead.	**Super-heavy Walker:** This model can Fall Back in the Movement phase and still shoot and/or charge in the same turn. When this model Falls Back, it can move over enemy **INFANTRY** and **SWARM** models, though it must end its move more than 1" from any enemy units. In addition, this model can move and fire Heavy weapons without suffering the penalty to its hit rolls. Finally, this model only gains a bonus to its save for being in cover if at least half of the model is obscured from the firer.

FACTION KEYWORDS	**IMPERIUM, IMPERIAL KNIGHTS, <QUESTOR ALLEGIANCE>, <HOUSEHOLD>**

KEYWORDS	**TITANIC, VEHICLE, DOMINUS CLASS, KNIGHT CASTELLAN**

A pair of redoubtable House Terryn Knights Castellan advance into battle, guns blazing.

KNIGHT VALIANT

NAME	M	WS	BS	S	T	W	A	Ld	Sv
Knight Valiant	*	*	*	8	8	28	4	9	3+

DAMAGE

Some of this model's characteristics change as it suffers damage, as shown below:

REMAINING W	M	WS	BS
15-28+	10"	4+	3+
8-14	7"	5+	4+
1-7	4"	6+	5+

A Knight Valiant is a single model equipped with a thundercoil harpoon, conflagration cannon, twin siegebreaker cannon, two twin meltaguns, four shieldbreaker missiles and titanic feet.

WEAPON	RANGE	TYPE	S	AP	D	ABILITIES
Conflagration cannon	18"	Heavy 3D6	7	-2	2	This weapon automatically hits its target.
Shieldbreaker missile	48"	Heavy 1	10	-4	D6	Each shieldbreaker missile can only be fired once per battle, and a model can only fire one each turn. Invulnerable saving throws cannot be made against wounds caused by this weapon.
Twin siegebreaker cannon	48"	Heavy 2D3	7	-1	D3	-
Thundercoil harpoon	12"	Heavy 1	16	-6	10	You can re-roll failed hit rolls when targeting **Vehicle** or **Monster** units with this weapon. In addition, if this weapon inflicts any damage, the target unit suffers an additional D3 mortal wounds.
Twin meltagun	12"	Assault 2	8	-4	D6	If the target is within half range of this weapon, roll two dice when inflicting damage with it and discard the lowest result.
Titanic feet	Melee	Melee	User	-2	D3	Make 3 hit rolls for each attack made with this weapon.

WARGEAR OPTIONS	• This model may replace two of its shieldbreaker missiles with a twin siegebreaker cannon.

ABILITIES	**Ion Shield:** This model has a 5+ invulnerable save against ranged weapons. **Dual Plasma Core Explosion:** If this model is reduced to 0 wounds, roll 2D6 before removing it from the battlefield. If you roll a 6 on either dice, it explodes, and each unit within 2D6" suffers D6 mortal wounds; if you roll a 6 on both dice, each unit within 3D6" suffers D6 mortal wounds instead.	**Super-heavy Walker:** This model can Fall Back in the Movement phase and still shoot and/or charge in the same turn. When this model Falls Back, it can move over enemy **Infantry** and **Swarm** models, though it must end its move more than 1" from any enemy units. In addition, this model can move and fire Heavy weapons without suffering the penalty to its hit rolls. Finally, this model only gains a bonus to its save for being in cover if at least half of the model is obscured from the firer.

FACTION KEYWORDS	IMPERIUM, IMPERIAL KNIGHTS, <Questor Allegiance>, <Household>

KEYWORDS	TITANIC, VEHICLE, DOMINUS CLASS, KNIGHT VALIANT

A Knight Valiant of House Raven leads the Imperial counter-attack, ready to immolate any foe that stands their ground.

Deployed at the forefront of battle, a Sacristan Forgeshrine forms a vital support hub for knightly lances.

4 POWER

SACRISTAN FORGESHRINE

A Sacristan Forgeshrine is a single model.

ABILITIES

Sector Mechanicus Structure: After it is set up, a Sacristan Forgeshrine is treated as a Sector Mechanicus terrain feature. It cannot move for any reason, is not treated as a friendly or enemy model, and cannot be targeted or affected by any attacks or abilities.

Unless they can **Fly**, **Vehicles**, **Monsters**, **Cavalry** and **Bikers** can only be set up and end their moves on the ground floor of a Sector Mechanicus Structure. Unless they can **Fly**, **Infantry**, **Beasts** and **Swarms** must scale ladders, girders or walls to ascend or descend between different levels of a Sector Mechanicus structure. **Infantry** are also assumed to be able to traverse around girders, buttresses and hanging chains, and so move through them without impediment.

Infantry units that are entirely on a Sector Mechanicus structure receive the bonus to their armour saves for being in cover (other units that are entirely on the structure only receive this bonus if at least 50% of every model is obscured from the point of view of the shooting unit).

Auto-Sacristan: At the end of your Movement phase, one **Imperial Knights Vehicle** from your army that is within 1" of this model can use the Forgeshrine's auto-Sacristan. If it does so, it cannot shoot or charge this turn and its Attacks characteristic is reduced to 1, but you can then choose and resolve one of the following effects:

- **Ritual of Repairing:** The vehicle regains D3 lost wounds. If there is a **Tech-Priest** or **Techmarine** from your army on the Sacristan Forgeshrine, and they have not used their ability to repair another vehicle this turn, they can aid in the ritual of repairing instead of using that ability this turn; if they do so, the vehicle regains 3 lost wounds instead.

- **Ritual of Reloading:** If the vehicle is equipped with shieldbreaker missiles, it regains all shieldbreaker missiles it fired previously in the battle. If it is not, or if it has its full complement of shieldbreaker missiles, choose one weapon the vehicle is equipped with (not an Heirloom of the Noble Houses). The next time it is fired, it always makes the maximum number of attacks (e.g. a Heavy 2D6 weapon will fire 12 shots).

- **Rite of Refuelling:** Until the end of your next Movement phase, increase the Move characteristic of the vehicle by 6".

A vehicle can only use an auto-Sacristan once per turn.

FACTION KEYWORDS	**Imperium, Imperial Knights**
KEYWORDS	**Sector Mechanicus, Sacristan Forgeshrine**

KNIGHTLY ARMAMENTS

The armouries of the Noble houses are replete with massive artillery guns, enormous energy cannons, racks of ballistic warheads and titanic melee weaponry. Even the smallest Knights wield several such weapons at once, acting as artillery platforms or assault vehicles capable of breaking the strength of entire enemy armies with their firepower and close-quarters fury.

RANGED WEAPONS

WEAPON	RANGE	TYPE	S	AP	D	ABILITIES
Archeotech pistol	15"	Pistol 1	5	-2	2	-
Armiger autocannon	60"	Heavy 2D3	7	-1	3	Ignore the penalty to hit rolls for moving and firing this Heavy weapon.
Avenger gatling cannon	36"	Heavy 12	6	-2	2	-
Conflagration cannon	18"	Heavy 3D6	7	-2	2	This weapon automatically hits its target.
Heavy flamer	8"	Heavy D6	5	-1	1	This weapon automatically hits its target.
Heavy stubber	36"	Heavy 3	4	0	1	-
Ironstorm missile pod	72"	Heavy D6	5	-1	2	This weapon can target units that are not visible to the bearer.
Las-impulsor	When attacking with this weapon, choose one of the profiles below.					
- Low intensity	36"	Heavy 2D6	6	-2	D3	-
- High intensity	18"	Heavy D6	12	-4	D6	-
Meltagun	12"	Assault 1	8	-4	D6	If the target is within half range of this weapon, roll two dice when inflicting damage with it and discard the lowest result.
Multi-laser	36"	Heavy 3	6	0	1	-
Plasma decimator	When attacking with this weapon, choose one of the profiles below.					
- Standard	48"	Heavy 2D6	7	-3	1	-
- Supercharge	48"	Heavy 2D6	8	-3	2	For each hit roll of 1, the bearer suffers 1 mortal wound after all of this weapon's shots have been resolved.
Rapid-fire battle cannon	72"	Heavy 2D6	8	-2	D3	-
Shieldbreaker missile	48"	Heavy 1	10	-4	D6	Each shieldbreaker missile can only be fired once per battle, and a model can only fire one each turn. Invulnerable saving throws cannot be made against wounds caused by a shieldbreaker missile.
Stormspear rocket pod	48"	Heavy 3	8	-2	D6	-
Thermal cannon	36"	Heavy D6	9	-4	D6	If the target is within half range of this weapon, roll two dice when inflicting damage with it and discard the lowest result.
Thermal spear	30"	Assault D3	8	-4	D6	If the target is within half range of this weapon, roll two dice when inflicting damage with it and discard the lowest result.
Thundercoil harpoon	12"	Heavy 1	16	-6	10	You can re-roll failed hit rolls when targeting **VEHICLE** or **MONSTER** units with this weapon. In addition, if this weapon inflicts any damage, the target unit suffers an additional D3 mortal wounds.
Twin Icarus autocannon	48"	Heavy 4	7	-1	2	Add 1 to all hit rolls made for this weapon against targets that can **FLY**. Subtract 1 from the hit rolls made for this weapon against all other targets.
Twin meltagun	12"	Assault 2	8	-4	D6	If the target is within half range of this weapon, roll two dice when inflicting damage with it and discard the lowest result.
Twin siegebreaker cannon	48"	Heavy 2D3	7	-1	D3	-
Volcano lance	80"	Heavy D6	14	-5	3D3	You can re-roll failed wound rolls when targeting **TITANIC** units with this weapon.

'The Omnissiah gifts us with his wrath made manifest, that we may turn it upon his foes with fulsome vengeance.'

- Sacristan Nymax Dar Mechanicus

MELEE WEAPONS

WEAPON	RANGE	TYPE	S	AP	D	ABILITIES
Freedom's Hand	Melee	Melee	x2	-4	2D6	When attacking with this weapon, you must subtract 1 from the hit roll. Treat any damage roll less than 6 made with this weapon as 6 instead. If a **Vehicle** or **Monster** is slain by this weapon, pick an enemy unit within 9" of the bearer and roll a D6. On a 4+ that unit suffers D3 mortal wounds.
Reaper chain-cleaver	When attacking with this weapon, choose one of the profiles below:					
- Strike	Melee	Melee	x2	-3	3	-
- Sweep	Melee	Melee	User	-2	1	Make 2 hit rolls for each attack made with this weapon, instead of 1.
Reaper chainsword	Melee	Melee	+6	-3	6	-
Thunderstrike gauntlet	Melee	Melee	x2	-4	6	When attacking with this weapon, you must subtract 1 from the hit roll. If a **Vehicle** or **Monster** is slain by this weapon, pick an enemy unit within 9" of the bearer and roll a D6. On a 4+ that unit suffers D3 mortal wounds.
Titanic feet	Melee	Melee	User	-2	D3	Make 3 hit rolls for each attack made with this weapon.

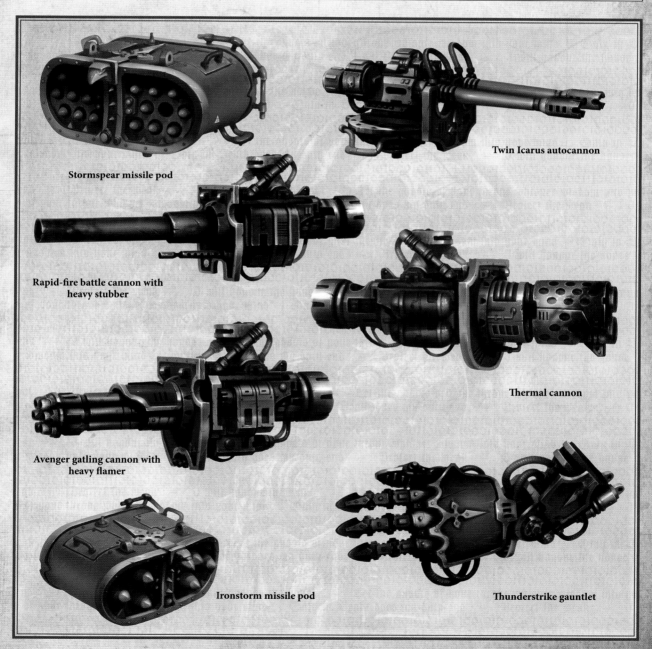

Stormspear missile pod

Twin Icarus autocannon

Rapid-fire battle cannon with heavy stubber

Thermal cannon

Avenger gatling cannon with heavy flamer

Ironstorm missile pod

Thunderstrike gauntlet

On the hive world of Palatoria, a horde of Bad Moons Orks attempts to surround the Knights of House Raven. They soon learn the magnitude of their error as the Knights, supported by Gerantius, smash through the greenskin lines in a storm of fire and blood.

MIGHT OF THE KNIGHT WORLDS

In this section you'll find rules for Battle-forged armies that include IMPERIAL KNIGHTS Detachments – that is, any Detachment which includes only IMPERIAL KNIGHTS units. These rules include the abilities below and a series of Stratagems that can only be used by the Imperial Knights. This section also includes the Imperial Knights' unique Warlord Traits, Relics and Tactical Objectives. Together, these rules reflect their character and fighting style in your games of Warhammer 40,000.

ABILITIES

IMPERIAL KNIGHTS Detachments (excluding Super-heavy Auxiliary Detachments) gain the following abilities:

KNIGHT LANCES

On the battlefield, Knights gather in formations called lances, earth-shaking spearheads of towering war engines led by the highest ranking amongst them.

If your army is Battle-forged, select one model in each IMPERIAL KNIGHTS Super-heavy Detachment in your army. Each model you selected gains the CHARACTER keyword. However, the Command Benefit of each Imperial Knights Super-heavy Detachment is changed to 'None' unless it contains any combination of at least three QUESTORIS CLASS and/or DOMINUS CLASS units.

HOUSEHOLD TRADITIONS

Knightly houses are ancient institutions with martial traditions that stretch back for millennia. Each fights in its own distinctive way.

If your army is Battle-forged, all units in an IMPERIAL KNIGHTS Super-heavy Detachment (other than FREEBLADE units) must be from the same Household, but they will all gain a Household Tradition (with the exception of FREEBLADE units, detailed opposite). The Household Tradition gained depends upon the household they are drawn from, as shown on the page opposite. For example, HOUSE TERRYN units with the Household Traditions ability gain the Gallant Warriors tradition.

If you have chosen a QUESTOR IMPERIALIS household that does not have an associated Household Tradition, you can choose the Questor Imperialis Household Tradition that

best describes the character and fighting style of your knightly house. Similarly, if you have chosen a QUESTOR MECHANICUS household that does not have an associated Household Tradition, you can choose the Questor Mechanicus Household Tradition that best describes the character and fighting style of your knightly house.

Freeblades

The inclusion of a FREEBLADE unit in an IMPERIAL KNIGHTS Detachment does not prevent other units in that Detachment from gaining a Household Tradition. However, FREEBLADE units can never themselves benefit from a Household Tradition.

'Every Knight world is a fortress, a mighty keep that watches over the worlds around it and illuminates the darkness with its blazing beacons. Just as the fortresses of the Noble houses provide protection for the serf classes that labour in their shadows, so the Knight worlds themselves provide protection for all other Imperial planets beneath their aegis. Never will loyal Knights shirk their duties in this regard.'

- Cernephalus, Sage Strategic of House Terryn

'AWAKEN, OH PLASMA GENERATOR, AND PUMP THINE BLOOD OF FIRE.

AWAKEN, OH CANNONS, OH ROCKETS, OH BLADES AND FISTS, AND PREPARE TO SMITE THE FOE.

AWAKEN, OH ION SHIELD, AND MUSTER THINE BASTION OF LIGHT.

AWAKEN, OH THRONE MECHANICUM. THE TIME FOR WAR HAS COME.'

- The Sacristans' Chant of Awakening

QUESTOR IMPERIALIS HOUSEHOLD TRADITIONS

HOUSE TERRYN: GALLANT WARRIORS
The Nobles of House Terryn are ever hungry for combat, driving their towering steeds hard across the field. The Knights are as eager as their pilots to take the fight to the foe, striding fleet and sure into the white heat of battle with ferocious determination.

When determining the distance that a unit with this Household Tradition Advances or charges, roll an additional D6 and discard the lowest result.

HOUSE GRIFFITH: GLORY OF THE CHARGE
Seeking supreme martial glory, the Nobles of House Griffith slam into the enemy formation like an avalanche. Their momentum and pitiless wrath are such that the foe are scattered before them like leaves upon a gale, their battle lines sundered by the apocalyptic charge of ironclad giants.

Add 1 to the Attacks characteristic of a model with this Household Tradition during any turn in which it charged or performed a Heroic Intervention. In addition, a model with this Household Tradition can perform Heroic Interventions as if it were a **Character**.

HOUSE HAWKSHROUD: OATHKEEPERS
The Nobles of Hawkshroud uphold the honour of their house above all, and refuse to yield whilst an oath remains unfulfilled.

Models with this Household Tradition double the number of wounds they have remaining for the purposes of determining what characteristics to use on their damage table.

HOUSE CADMUS: HUNTERS OF THE FOE
House Cadmus' Knights are accomplished at wading through hordes of lesser enemies, culling them like vermin.

Re-roll wound rolls of 1 in the Fight phase for attacks made by models with this Household Tradition against units which only contain models with a Wounds characteristic of 12 or less.

HOUSE MORTAN: CLOSE-QUARTERS KILLERS
The Nobles of House Mortan are hardened and merciless, preferring to finish their foes with fist and blade.

Add 1 to hit rolls in the Fight phase for attacks made by a model with this Household Tradition during any turn in which it charged, was charged, or performed a Heroic Intervention.

QUESTOR MECHANICUS HOUSEHOLD TRADITIONS

HOUSE RAVEN: RELENTLESS ADVANCE
The Knights of House Raven grind inexorably forwards, hammering their enemies with fire all the while.

Models with this Household Tradition do not suffer the penalties to their hit rolls for Advancing and firing Assault weapons. Furthermore, during a turn in which a unit with this Household Tradition Advances, all of its Heavy weapons are treated as Assault weapons (e.g. a Heavy 3 weapon is treated as an Assault 3 weapon).

HOUSE TARANIS: OMNISSIAH'S GRACE
No Noble house is higher in the Omnissiah's favour than Taranis. They enjoy his singular blessings.

Roll a dice each time a model with this Household Tradition loses a wound, unless that wound was lost as the result of a mortal wound; on a 6 the wound being rolled for is not lost.

HOUSE KRAST: COLD FURY
The Knights of House Krast are fuelled by their rage, which burns hottest when faced by the most dread of foes.

You can re-roll failed hit rolls in the Fight phase for a model with this Household Tradition during any turn in which it charged, was charged, or performed a Heroic Intervention. In addition, you can re-roll all failed hit rolls in the Fight phase for a model with this Household Tradition against **Titanic** units.

HOUSE VULKER: FIRESTORM PROTOCOLS
House Vulker fight from afar with coldly methodical logic, targeting and eliminating their enemies with steely efficiency before they can ever reach friendly lines.

Re-roll hit rolls of 1 for a model with this Household Tradition whenever you are resolving an attack with a ranged weapon that is targeting the closest enemy unit.

STRATAGEMS

If your army is Battle-forged and includes any IMPERIAL KNIGHTS Detachments, you have access to the Stratagems shown below, meaning you can spend Command Points to activate them. These help to reflect the unique tactics and strategies used by the Imperial Knights on the battlefield. Some of the Stratagems listed here are unique to specific knightly houses.

ION AEGIS
2CP

Imperial Knights Stratagem

Redirecting power from its secondary plasma core, the Dominus-class Knight projects its ion shield over nearby allies.

Use this Stratagem at the start of your opponent's Movement phase. Choose a **DOMINUS CLASS** unit from your army. That unit cannot move until the end of its next turn for any reason, but until the start of your next turn, friendly **IMPERIUM** units have a 5+ invulnerable save against ranged weapons whilst they are wholly within 6" of that unit.

NOBLE SACRIFICE
2CP

Imperial Knights Stratagem

Sensing their end drawing close, the pilot overloads their Knight's plasma core to take the enemy with them.

Use this Stratagem before rolling to see if an **IMPERIAL KNIGHTS** model from your army explodes. If it is an **ARMIGER CLASS** or **QUESTORIS CLASS** model, it explodes on a roll of 4+. If it is a **DOMINUS CLASS** model, it explodes if either roll is 4+; if both rolls are 4+ then all units within 3D6" are affected.

THUNDERSTOMP
1CP

Imperial Knights Stratagem

The Knight brings its foot crashing down with the force of an industrial piledriver. Few can survive such a blow.

Use this Stratagem immediately after fighting with a **TITANIC IMPERIAL KNIGHTS** model from your army. Choose an enemy **INFANTRY** or **SWARM** unit within 1" of that model and roll a dice; on a 4+ the enemy unit suffers D3 mortal wounds.

SKYREAPER PROTOCOLS
1CP

Imperial Knights Stratagem

The Armiger Helverin's pilot intones prayers to the machine spirits of their autocannons, beseeching them to guide their aim against fast-moving airborne targets.

Use this Stratagem in your Shooting phase before an **ARMIGER HELVERIN** from your army makes its attacks against an enemy unit that can **FLY**. Until the end of the phase, you can re-roll failed hit rolls for that Armiger Helverin's Armiger autocannons against that enemy unit.

ROTATE ION SHIELDS
1CP/3CP

Imperial Knights Stratagem

Veteran Knight pilots can swiftly angle their ion shields to better deflect incoming fire.

Use this Stratagem when an enemy unit targets an **IMPERIAL KNIGHTS VEHICLE** unit from your army that has an invulnerable save (this Stratagem costs 3 CPs if the targeted unit is a **DOMINUS CLASS** unit, otherwise it costs 1 CP). Until the end of the phase, that vehicle unit's invulnerable save is improved by 1 (to a maximum of 3+).

HEIRLOOMS OF THE HOUSEHOLD
1CP/3CP

Imperial Knights Stratagem

The catacombs beneath many knightly strongholds delve deep, and are replete with ancient technological wonders.

Use this Stratagem before the battle. Choose one **QUESTORIS CLASS** or **DOMINUS CLASS** model from your army for 1 CP, or choose two such models for 3 CP. Each model you chose gains the **CHARACTER** keyword and can have one Heirloom of the Noble Houses. All of the Heirlooms of the Noble Houses that your army includes must be different and be given to different **IMPERIAL KNIGHTS CHARACTERS**. You can only use this Stratagem once per battle.

EXALTED COURT
1CP/3CP

Imperial Knights Stratagem

It is a truly glorious day for the Imperium when the Exalted Court takes to the battlefield. Led by their liege, these storied heroes bring wisdom and strength in equal measure.

Use this Stratagem before the battle, after you have chosen your Warlord. Choose one **QUESTORIS CLASS** or **DOMINUS CLASS** model from your army for 1 CP, or choose two such models for 3 CP. Each model you chose gains the **CHARACTER** keyword, and you can choose an Imperial Knights Warlord Trait for them (note that this model is only regarded as your Warlord for the purposes of this Warlord Trait). All of the Imperial Knights Warlord Traits in your army must be different (if randomly generated, re-roll duplicate results), and no model can have more than one. You can only use this Stratagem once per battle.

PACK HUNTERS
1CP

Imperial Knights Stratagem

Armiger Warglaives fight like hunting hounds; once one has engaged the enemy and brought them to bay, the rest of the pack swiftly falls upon the hapless victims.

Use this Stratagem after a <Household> Armiger Warglaive from your army has charged. Until the end of the phase, you can re-roll failed charge rolls for friendly <Household> Armiger Warglaives whilst they are within 12" of that model.

OATHBREAKER GUIDANCE SYSTEM
2CP

Imperial Knights Stratagem

The Noble houses claim that the machine spirits of their shieldbreaker missiles can scent dishonour, hunting out those who would hide behind their thralls and explosively punishing them for their cowardice.

Use this Stratagem before choosing a target for a shieldbreaker missile in your Shooting phase. That shieldbreaker missile can target a unit that is not visible to its bearer, and can target a Character even if it is not the closest enemy unit.

FULL TILT
2CP

Imperial Knights Stratagem

With the enemy before them, their Knight's machine spirit snarling, and the rush of battle coursing through their veins, the Noble pilot pours power into their motive actuators and thunders into the fight.

Use this Stratagem in your Charge phase. Choose an Imperial Knights Vehicle from your army that Advanced this turn. That model can declare a charge even though it Advanced this turn.

IRONHAIL HEAVY STUBBERS
1CP

Questor Imperialis Stratagem

A technology recently adopted from the wider Imperium after centuries of Sacristan mistrust, these upgraded heavy stubbers slice through enemy armour with their fire.

Use this Stratagem before the battle. Choose one Imperial Knights Detachment from your army. The AP characteristic of all heavy stubbers equipped on Questor Imperialis models in that Detachment is changed to -1.

DEVASTATING REACH
1CP

Imperial Knights Stratagem

Even cowering in ruined buildings or climbing to towering heights cannot save the enemy from their just fate.

Use this Stratagem in your Charge phase. Choose a Titanic Imperial Knights model from your army that has not yet charged, then choose one enemy unit that is entirely on ruins or a Sector Mechanicus structure (and none of its models are on the ground floor) as the target of its charge. If your model can end its charge move within 2" horizontally and 6" vertically of that enemy unit, the charge is successful and you can make close combat attacks against it in the ensuing Fight phase (all hit rolls made using titanic feet automatically fail). If you cannot end your charge move within the above mentioned distances, the charge fails.

CHAINSWEEP
1CP

Imperial Knights Stratagem

With a snarl, the Noble swings their Knight's chainsword in a howling arc that rips through the enemy ranks and sends sundered foes tumbling through the blood-misted air.

Use this Stratagem immediately after fighting with an Imperial Knights model from your army that is equipped with a reaper chainsword, Ravager or Honour's Bite. Roll a D6 for each enemy model within 3" of that model; on a 6 that enemy model's unit suffers a mortal wound.

DEATH GRIP
1CP

Imperial Knights Stratagem

The servo-articulated digits of the Knight's fist close around the victim with piston pressure and begin to squeeze…

Use this Stratagem immediately after fighting with an Imperial Knights model from your army that is equipped with a thunderstrike gauntlet, the Paragon Gauntlet or Freedom's Hand. Resolve an additional attack with that weapon against an enemy unit within 1" that consists of a single model. If the attack hits, the enemy model suffers D3 mortal wounds instead of the normal damage and is caught in a death grip: both players roll off and add their respective model's Strength characteristic to their result. If your opponent's result equals or exceeds yours, the enemy model breaks free and nothing happens; otherwise, the enemy model suffers an additional D3 mortal wounds and both players roll off again as before. Continue to do this until either the enemy model breaks free or it is slain.

BONDED OATHSMEN
Imperial Knights Stratagem

1CP

Knights who have been neurally bonded to Armiger pilots will often call upon them to charge to their aid, turning the tables on the attacking foe.

Use this Stratagem at the end of the enemy Charge phase. Choose a <HOUSEHOLD> QUESTORIS CLASS or DOMINUS CLASS unit from your army that has been charged this turn. All friendly <HOUSEHOLD> ARMIGER CLASS units that are within 6" of that unit can immediately perform a Heroic Intervention as if they were CHARACTERS; each can move up to 6" when doing so, and must end its move closer to the nearest enemy unit.

VALIANT LAST STAND
Questor Imperialis Stratagem

2CP

Badly wounded, their Knight's generator on the verge of overload, still the Noble fights on, drawing upon their reserves of chivalric heroism to sell their life as dearly as they can.

Use this Stratagem when a QUESTOR IMPERIALIS model from your army is reduced to 0 wounds but did not explode. Before removing it from the battlefield, that model can immediately either shoot as if it were your Shooting phase or fight as if it were your Fight phase. When resolving these attacks, assume the model has 1 wound remaining when determining which characteristics to use on its damage table.

BENEVOLENCE OF THE MACHINE GOD
Questor Mechanicus Stratagem

1CP

As the forces of the enemy rain destruction down upon the Knight, its Noble pilot offers up a binharic prayer to the Omnissiah for protection.

Use this Stratagem when a QUESTOR MECHANICUS model from your army suffers a mortal wound. Roll a D6 for that mortal wound and each other mortal wound inflicted on that model for the rest of the phase: on a 5+ the mortal wound being rolled for is ignored.

MACHINE SPIRIT RESURGENT
Questor Mechanicus Stratagem

1CP

Through the broadcasting of auto-sequenced data-hymnals, the pilot reinvigorates their Knight's machine spirit, stoking its predatory ire and directing it at the foe.

Use this Stratagem at the start of any turn. Pick a QUESTOR MECHANICUS unit from your army. Until the end of this turn, use the top row of the model's damage table, regardless of how many wounds it has left. This ends immediately if the model is reduced to 0 wounds.

COGNIS HEAVY STUBBERS
Questor Mechanicus Stratagem

1CP

The machine spirits of these heavy stubbers independently target incoming foes and provide excellent point-defence.

Use this Stratagem before the battle. Choose one IMPERIAL KNIGHTS Detachment in your army. All heavy stubbers equipped on QUESTOR MECHANICUS models in that Detachment gain the following ability: 'You can fire this weapon even if the bearer Advanced this turn, but you must subtract 2 from the hit rolls if you do so. When firing Overwatch with this weapon, the attacks are resolved using the firing model's Ballistic Skill. You can re-roll failed hit rolls for this weapon if the bearer Advanced this turn and has the Relentless Advance Household Tradition (pg 107), or if the bearer is firing Overwatch and has the Firestorm Protocols Household Tradition (pg 107).'

SALLY FORTH!
Questor Imperialis Stratagem

3CP

The aggressive temperaments of most Nobles, coupled with the long stride of their Knights, leads many lances to employ dynamic strategies to swiftly outflank the foe.

Use this Stratagem during deployment. You can send one QUESTOR IMPERIALIS QUESTORIS CLASS or ARMIGER CLASS unit from your army to outflank the enemy instead of setting it up on the battlefield. At the end of any of your Movement phases this unit can join the battle – set it up so that it is within 6" of any battlefield edge and more than 9" away from any enemy models. You can only use this Stratagem once per battle.

SLAYERS OF SHADOWS
House Mortan Stratagem

1CP

Used to fighting in the dark, House Mortan Nobles close their eyes and let their ancestors' whispers guide their aim.

Use this Stratagem in your Shooting phase before choosing a HOUSE MORTAN unit from your army to shoot with. Until the end of the phase, that unit ignores all modifiers (positive and negative) when making its attacks.

GLORY IN HONOUR!
House Terryn Stratagem

3CP

Drawing upon the heroism that is their birthright, inspired by the spirits of the Noble ancients within their Throne Mechanicum, the pilot unleashes their full fury upon the foe.

Use this Stratagem after a HOUSE TERRYN unit from your army has fought in the Fight phase. That unit can fight an additional time this phase.

ORDER OF COMPANIONS
House Raven Stratagem

The Order of Companions use little in the way of visible markings to denote their elite status, but instead maintain a constant stream of noospheric communication to aid each other in battle. The first warning most enemies receive that such elite warriors are coordinating their demise is when a deadly-accurate volley of fire tears through their ranks.

Use this Stratagem at the start of your Shooting phase. Pick a **House Raven** model from your army. Until the end of the phase, re-roll all rolls of 1 for that model (this includes hit rolls, wound rolls, damage rolls and rolls made to determine the number of shots fired by weapons that make a random number of attacks).

2CP

OUR DARKEST HOUR
House Taranis Stratagem

House Taranis were almost annihilated once before. The same tenacity that saved them then still runs in the blood of their Nobles and the mechanical veins of their Knights.

Use this Stratagem when a **House Taranis** model from your army is reduced to 0 wounds but did not explode. Roll a D6; on a 4+ set the model up again at the end of the phase, as close as possible to its previous position and more than 1" from any enemies, with D3 wounds remaining.

2CP

SATURATION BOMBARDMENT
House Vulker Stratagem

The saturation bombardments of House Vulker are infamous, their Nobles elevating their guns and letting fly on pre-cogitated trajectories. The enemy are caught in a firestorm as the Omnissiah's wrath rains down upon them.

Use this Stratagem in your Shooting phase before choosing a **House Vulker** model from your army to shoot with. Until the end of the phase, each unmodified hit roll of 6 made for that model's shooting attacks scores 2 hits instead of 1.

1CP

DRAGONSLAYER
House Griffith Stratagem

The Nobles of House Griffith have a long and proud history of ruthlessly hunting down and expertly slaying the most monstrous of foes.

Use this Stratagem before a **House Griffith** model from your army makes its attacks in the Shooting or Fight phase. Until the end of the phase, add 1 to wound rolls made for that model's attacks against units containing models with a Wounds characteristic of 10 or more.

2CP

CONTROLLED AGGRESSION
House Krast Stratagem

When the Knights of House Krast enter close-quarters combat, they do so certain in the knowledge that their attack speed and aggression protocols are optimal.

Use this Stratagem in the Fight phase before choosing a **House Krast** unit to fight with. Until the end of the phase, each unmodified hit roll of 6 made for that unit's attacks scores 2 hits instead of 1, or 3 hits instead of 1 if the target is a **Chaos** unit. A model cannot be affected by both the Controlled Aggression Stratagem and the Thunderstomp, Death Grip or Chainsweep Stratagems in the same turn.

1CP

BIO-SCRYER COGITATOR ARRAY
House Cadmus Stratagem

Some Knights of Cadmus mount specialised cogitator arrays within their cockpits, technology salvaged from Gryphonne IV that allows them to track their prey via bio-signatures.

Use this Stratagem immediately after your opponent sets up a unit that is arriving on the battlefield as reinforcements within 12" of a **House Cadmus** model from your army. That model can immediately shoot at that enemy unit as if it were your Shooting phase.

3CP

STAUNCH ALLIES
House Hawkshroud Stratagem

So ingrained is House Hawkshroud's reputation for loyalty that they won't hesitate to come to an ally's aid, opening fire with their guns before storming in to join the fray.

Use this Stratagem immediately after an enemy unit declares a charge against an **Imperium** unit from your army. Choose a friendly **House Hawkshroud** model that is more than 1" from any enemy units and within 12" of the unit that is the target of the charge. That model fires Overwatch at the charging unit as if it were itself targeted by the charge. Furthermore, if the resulting charge is successful, that model can perform a Heroic Intervention against the unit that charged at the end of the phase as if it were a **Character**; if it does so it can move up to 2D6", but must end this move closer to the unit that charged and cannot move within 1" of any other enemy unit.

2CP

WARLORD TRAITS

The Barons of the Questor Imperialis worlds are masterful tacticians and bellicose warriors, whilst the Princeps of the Questor Mechanicus Knight houses are augmetically enhanced martial savants. In either case, their command of their forces is absolute, and their performance in battle is awe-inspiring to behold.

If an **IMPERIAL KNIGHTS CHARACTER** is your Warlord, you can generate a Warlord Trait for them from the table below. Note that Imperial Knights Warlords cannot take Warlord Traits from the *Warhammer 40,000* rulebook. You can either roll on the table to randomly generate a Warlord Trait, or you can select the one that best suits their style of waging war. If Canis Rex has a Warlord Trait, both **CANIS REX** and **SIR HEKHTUR** will have Fearsome Reputation.

D6 RESULT

1 CUNNING COMMANDER

This Warlord is a master tactician, and instinctively knows how best to use the battlefield to their advantage.

Once per battle, you can re-roll one hit roll, wound roll, damage roll or saving throw made for your Warlord. In addition, if your army is Battle-forged, you gain an additional Command Point.

2 ION BULWARK

A survivor of countless battles, this Warlord has learnt to angle their Knight suit's ion shield with exceptional deftness.

Your Warlord has a 4+ invulnerable save against ranged weapons.

3 KNIGHT SENESCHAL

Veteran warriors who have proved themselves worthy time and again in the fires of battle are awarded the rank of Knight Seneschal. To be named so is an honour beyond measure. Either through countless martial triumphs or by one truly heroic act, this Warlord has distinguished themselves above and beyond their peers and is a true paragon of their house.

Add 1 to your Warlord's Attacks characteristic.

4 LANDSTRIDER

This Warlord has fought across hundreds of battlefields, and is an expert at reading strat-map inloads and coordinating their forces' advance.

Add 2 to all Advance and charge rolls made for friendly <**HOUSEHOLD**> units within 6" of your Warlord.

5 BLESSED BY THE SACRISTANS

This Warlord bears a token of the favour of the Sacristans in the form of an artificer weapon of unrivalled quality.

Choose one weapon (not an Heirloom of the Noble Houses) that your Warlord is equipped with. Each time you make an unmodified wound roll of 6 for that weapon, the target suffers a mortal wound in addition to the normal damage.

6 FEARSOME REPUTATION

The deeds of this Knight are known across the galaxy, and all know that to confront it is to face certain death.

Enemy units must subtract 1 from their Leadership characteristic whilst they are within 12" of your Warlord. Whilst they are within 6" of your Warlord, subtract 2 from their Leadership instead.

HOUSEHOLD WARLORD TRAITS

If you wish, you can pick a Household Warlord Trait from the list below instead of the Imperial Knight Warlord Traits opposite, but only if your Warlord is from the relevant household.

HOUSEHOLD	TRAIT
Terryn	**Champion of the Household:** *Terryn's rulers can always be found at the forefront of their house's armies.* You can re-roll failed charge rolls for your Warlord.
Griffith	**Master of the Joust:** *The lords of Griffith are experts at striking pinpoint blows while at full stride.* Immediately after your Warlord completes a charge move, choose one enemy unit within 1" and roll a D6: on a 4+ that unit suffers D3 mortal wounds.
Hawkshroud	**Duty of the Forsworn:** *The champions of Hawkshroud often take to the field having sworn a binding oath to slay a particular foe.* At the start of the first battle round, but before the first turn begins, select one unit in your opponent's army. Add 1 to hit rolls made for your Warlord against that unit.
Cadmus	**Veteran of Gryphonne IV:** *Those Knights of Cadmus who survived the destruction of Gryphonne IV by Hive Fleet Leviathan proved their endurance time and again.* Reduce all damage suffered by your Warlord in the Fight phase by 1 (to a minimum of 1).
Mortan	**Legacy of the Black Pall:** *The gloom of their home world of Kimdaria seems to cling to the Knights of House Mortan.* Subtract 1 from hit rolls for attacks that target your Warlord at a range of more than 18".
Raven	**Master of the Trial:** *Those elite Nobles who emerge triumphant from House Raven's Trial of the Companions are forever hardened by the experience.* Add 1 to saving throws made for your Warlord against attacks that have an AP characteristic of -1 (this does not affect invulnerable saving throws).
Taranis	**Knight of Mars:** *The data-manifolds of House Taranis' lords are thrice-blessed by the priests of the Red Planet.* Each time you make a wound roll of 6+ for your Warlord in the Shooting phase, the AP characteristic of that attack is improved by 1 (e.g. AP0 becomes AP-1).
Krast	**First Knight:** *As exemplars of the first rediscovered Noble house, the leaders of Krast constantly strive to uphold a long and glorious history.* Re-roll hit rolls of 1 for your Warlord.
Vulker	**Adamantium Knight:** *The most accomplished of House Vulker's Knights are fitted with a sub-layer of adamantine weave.* Wound rolls of 1, 2 or 3 made for attacks against your Warlord always fail, even if the attack has a Strength characteristic higher than your Warlord's Toughness characteristic.

'Logic dictates that the greatest concentration of force shall yield victory. Thus, logically, our enemies stand no chance whatsoever of defeating us.'

- Baron-logisticor Artemoris Raven

HEIRLOOMS OF THE NOBLE HOUSES

The ancient heirlooms of the Knight worlds are echoes of a bygone age. Some have endured since the first ships of the Long March colonised space in M15, and all are peerless examples of the artificer's craft, superlative objects of ornate wargear whose might can turn the tide of battle.

If your army is led by an **IMPERIAL KNIGHTS** Warlord, then before the battle you may give one of the following Heirlooms of the Noble Houses to an **IMPERIAL KNIGHTS CHARACTER**. Named characters such as Canis Rex already have one or more artefacts and cannot be given any of the following heirlooms.

Note that some weapons replace one of the unit's existing weapons. Where this is the case, if you are playing a matched play game or are otherwise using points values, you must still pay the cost of the weapon that is being replaced. Write down any Heirlooms of the Noble Houses your units have on your army roster.

SANCTUARY

Despite whispers of xenos taint in its origins, the potent ion shield generator known as Sanctuary is a venerated war relic. Through the projection of rapidly modulating and overlapping energy fields, coupled with a steady emission of warding incense and a cycling barrage of data-hymnals, this device wards away the furious fire of the enemy. It does not even require tilting and angling like a typical ion shield, for its effects wreathe the Knight suit in an all-encompassing field of protective energies and holy wards. The resultant field clings to the Knight like an energised second skin, flexing and shifting with its movement and protecting it from even close-quarters attacks.

The bearer has a 5+ invulnerable save against ranged and melee weapons.

RAVAGER

This storied reaper chainsword has claimed millions of lives during its long service to the knightly houses. The chainsword's razor-sharp teeth were harvested from the canines of a long-extinct species of bio-horror called a Balethrox. What makes this fact so startling is that dozens of the fell creatures must have been hunted down and slain by brave Knights in order to secure enough fangs to line Ravager's cutting blade. However, witnessing the murderous wrath of this chainblade's touch in battle more than justifies the dedication of those long-dead Knights, and its bearer will fight all the harder to honour their sacrifice.

Model with a reaper chainsword only. Ravager replaces the bearer's reaper chainsword and has the following profile:

WEAPON	RANGE	TYPE	S	AP	D
Ravager	Melee	Melee	+8	-4	6
Abilities: Re-roll hit rolls of 1 for this weapon. If the bearer has the Cold Fury Household Tradition (pg 107), you can instead re-roll all failed hit rolls for this weapon.					

THE PARAGON GAUNTLET

It is believed that this masterwork weapon was the prototype for the thunderstrike gauntlet – the first, perfect copy fabricated by a long-lost STC that was developed on Mars during the Age of Technology. It was that same STC that was integral to the founding of the Knight worlds themselves, by equipping Mankind's first colonisation fleets with the knowledge to build the mighty armoured suits. If true, it would certainly explain the incredible level of artifice that went into the gauntlet's creation.

Model with a thunderstrike gauntlet only. The Paragon Gauntlet replaces the bearer's thunderstrike gauntlet and has the following profile:

WEAPON	RANGE	TYPE	S	AP	D
The Paragon Gauntlet	Melee	Melee	x2	-4	8
Abilities: If a **VEHICLE** or **MONSTER** is slain by this weapon, pick an enemy unit within 9" of the bearer and roll a D6. On a 4+ that unit suffers D3 mortal wounds.					

ARMOUR OF THE SAINTED ION

This exceptionally crafted carapace bodyglove is worn by the Noble pilot. It is studded with secondary couplings and electrosockets that couple with the machineries of the Throne Mechanicum in a similar fashion to the pilot's neural jacks. Once bonded in this fashion, the micro-generators within the armour thrum to life. They project streams of ionic energy, not only wreathing the pilot and their Throne in a protective shield, but reinforcing and protecting the Knight's internal systems. Thus, even shots and blows that penetrate the outer shell of the Knight's armour may fail to cause any harm.

The wearer's Knight has a Save characteristic of 2+.

ENDLESS FURY

This remarkable avenger gatling cannon is fitted with ballistic micro-fabricators that churn out fresh ammunition as fast as it can be fired. Rumours persist of the weapon's wielders being driven slowly mad with bloodlust, but even if there is truth to these claims, it is seen as a small price to pay for the power unleashed.

Model with an avenger gatling cannon only. Endless Fury replaces the bearer's avenger gatling cannon and has the following profile:

WEAPON	RANGE	TYPE	S	AP	D
Endless Fury	36"	Heavy 14	6	-2	2
Abilities: Each unmodified hit roll of 6 made with this weapon scores 2 hits instead of 1.					

JUDGEMENT

This unique rocket pod fires self-propelled adamantine tipped warheads fitted with servitor brains and running venatoris auto-targeting protocols. Once launched, these projectiles mercilessly hunt their prey across the battlefield.

Model with a stormspear rocket pod only. Judgement replaces the bearer's stormspear rocket pod and has the following profile:

WEAPON	RANGE	TYPE	S	AP	D
Judgement	60"	Heavy 3	8	-3	D6
Abilities: You can re-roll failed hit rolls for this weapon.					

SKYSHIELD

These formidable Icarus autocannons boast auto-predictive targeting cogitators and a vengeful machine spirit whose eternal vigilance is well proven.

Model with a twin Icarus autocannon only. Skyshield replaces the bearer's twin Icarus autocannon and has the following profile:

WEAPON	RANGE	TYPE	S	AP	D
Skyshield	60"	Heavy 6	7	-2	2
Abilities: Add 1 to all hit rolls made for this weapon against targets that can **FLY**. Subtract 1 from the hit rolls for this weapon against all other targets.					

HELM OF THE NAMELESS WARRIOR

Though many great heroes through the ages have mounted this fabled faceplate upon their Knight suits, the names of both the suit and the valiant pilot who first bore this helm have been lost to history. Regardless of its origins, the Helm of the Nameless Warrior has become synonymous with murderous ferocity in battle.

QUESTOR IMPERIALIS model only. Add 1 to hit rolls made for the wearer's attacks in the Fight phase.

BANNER OF MACHARIUS TRIUMPHANT

A gift from Lord Solar Macharius himself to honour the knightly houses that accompanied his crusade, this banner was borne to battle by a Knight Seneschal in every engagement in which the Knights fought alongside the Warmaster. Legend has it that the Banner of Macharius Triumphant has never seen defeat: every time a Knight has carried it to war, a great victory has been won for the Imperium. To see its majestic form fluttering in the wind instils the Emperor's warriors with great courage, for to fight in its shadow is to all but assure victory.

QUESTOR IMPERIALIS QUESTORIS CLASS model only. Add 1 to the Leadership characteristic of friendly **IMPERIUM** units within 6" of the bearer. In addition, if the bearer is within range of an objective marker (as specified in the mission), it controls that objective marker even if there are more enemy models within range of the same objective marker. If an enemy unit within range of the same objective marker has a similar ability, then the objective marker is controlled by the player who has the most models within range of it as normal – in this case, however, the bearer counts as 10 models.

TRAITOR'S PYRE

This ornate conflagration cannon was borne upon a three-hundred-and-fifty year pilgrimage to the cardinal world of Basphoria, so that it might be blessed by Saint Gauschwyn the Wrathful. The saint's spiritual influence fortified the weapon's machine spirit and greatly enhanced its ferocity, imparting a portion of Gauschwyn's infamous wrath upon it.

QUESTOR IMPERIALIS model with a conflagration cannon only. Traitor's Pyre replaces the bearer's conflagration cannon and has the following profile:

WEAPON	RANGE	TYPE	S	AP	D
Traitor's Pyre	18"	Heavy 3D6	7	-2	2
Abilities: This weapon automatically hits its target. You can re-roll failed wound rolls for this weapon.					

MARK OF THE OMNISSIAH

A device forged in the shape of the cog of Mars, the Mark of the Omnissiah is an incredibly potent self-repair hub. If the Knight suit upon which it is affixed takes battle damage, reconstruction protocols automatically engage to repair rents and restore lost power.

QUESTOR MECHANICUS model only. Roll a D6 at the start of your turn. On a 6 the bearer regains D3 lost wounds; on any other result it regains 1 lost wound.

THE HELM DOMINATUS

This noospheric interface emits a temporary cerebral override that summons nearby bonded Armigers to aid the bearer.

QUESTORIS MECHANICUS <HOUSEHOLD> QUESTORIS CLASS or **DOMINUS CLASS** model only. Once per battle round, at the start of either your Shooting phase or Fight phase, you can choose a unit from your opponent's army that is within 24" of the bearer. Until the end of the phase, add 1 to hit rolls for attacks made by **<HOUSEHOLD> ARMIGER CLASS** models against that enemy unit whilst they are within 6" of the bearer.

CAWL'S WRATH

During his centuries-long efforts to reduce the size and increase the portability of advanced plasma weaponry, Archmagos Cawl created this singular plasma decimator. Its enhanced containment fields and machine spirit data-shackles allow it to generate even more lethal volumes of energy than a typical example of such a weapon.

QUESTOR MECHANICUS model with a plasma decimator only. Cawl's Wrath replaces the bearer's plasma decimator and has the following profile:

WEAPON	RANGE	TYPE	S	AP	D
Cawl's Wrath (standard)	48"	Heavy 2D6	8	-4	2
Cawl's Wrath (supercharge)	48"	Heavy 2D6	9	-4	3

Abilities: When attacking with this weapon, choose one of the profiles above. When firing the supercharge profile, for each hit roll of 1, the bearer suffers 1 mortal wound after all of this weapon's shots have been resolved.

THUNDER OF VOLTORIS

Originally, Thunder of Voltoris was a defensive cannon mounted upon the battlements of House Terryn's mountainous stronghold. During the Khybus Schism, the traitors of the Sevenskull Cult attempted to assassinate the house's ruler as he walked beyond the safety of his fortress walls. Thunder of Voltoris is said to have fired of its own volition, a miraculous discharge that slew the traitors in a ball of flame and saved High King Nathanial. To honour the weapon's machine spirit, Nathanial had the artillery piece removed and fashioned into a battle cannon that could be borne to glory by his scions until the end of days.

HOUSE TERRYN model with rapid-fire battle cannon only. The Thunder of Voltoris replaces the bearer's rapid-fire battle cannon and has the following profile:

WEAPON	RANGE	TYPE	S	AP	D
The Thunder of Voltoris	72"	Heavy 2D6	9	-2	D3

Abilities: When determining how many shots this weapon fires, roll 3D6 and discard the lowest result.

MARK OF THE LANCE

A Noble who has won victory in the fabled Field of Adamantium tourney earns the right to bear this unique mark of honour into battle. Micro-circuitry woven into the honour pennant sends jolts of electrical force surging through the Knight's melee weaponry, enhancing the pilot's already proven skill in one-to-one combat.

HOUSE GRIFFITH model only. Each time the bearer completes a charge move, choose an enemy unit within 1" of it and roll a D6. On a 2+ that unit suffers D3 mortal wounds; on a 6 it suffers 3 mortal wounds instead.

ANGEL'S GRACE

This gilded halo fits into the data-couplings atop a Throne Mechanicum. It was crafted by the artificers of the Blood Angels Chapter to honour a debt to one of House Hawkshroud's devoted Knights who fought alongside them on Theska II. Unnatural manifestations of empyric power, the malefic conjurations of damned sorcerers, and all other forms of foul witchery are warded away by the Angel's Grace, lending credence to the claim that whoever sits their Throne beneath the ornate device enjoys the personal protection of the Primarch Sanguinius himself.

HOUSE HAWKSHROUD model only. Roll a D6 each time the bearer suffers a mortal wound in your opponent's psychic phase; on a 4+ the wound being rolled for is not lost.

THE HUNTER'S EYE

This remarkable data-manifold was recovered by the Nobles of House Cadmus almost eight millennia ago, during a crusade amidst the blighted tech-graves of Kossok's World. It surrounds a Noble's Throne with a remarkable holo-projected bio-scan and engine-signature readout whose gaze penetrates the densest terrain as though it were not there. Thus, the pilot is able to direct their fury against even those enemies who believe themselves wholly safe and undetected.

HOUSE CADMUS model only. Enemy units do not receive the bonus to their saving throws for cover against the bearer's ranged attacks.

HONOUR'S BITE

Honour's Bite was fashioned by a conclave of artificer-magi from the forge world of Ionus X. It was created as payment for the heroic sacrifice of High King Garthalomew Mortan, who stood alone in his Knight Paladin Lord of the Hunt against three enraged Squiggoths during the Dastorvol evacuation. Garthalomew successfully held off the trio of greenskin beasts, slaying the third even as it laid him low. In the process, he protected the entire tech-magi conclave of Dastorvol, allowing them to escape their overrun planet without a single casualty. Garthalomew's descendants have wielded Honour's Bite in his name ever since.

HOUSE MORTAN model with a reaper chainsword only. Honour's Bite replaces the bearer's reaper chainsword and has the following profile:

WEAPON	RANGE	TYPE	S	AP	D
Honour's Bite	Melee	Melee	+6	-4	6

Abilities: Each wound roll of 6 made for this weapon inflicts D3 mortal wounds on the target in addition to the normal damage.

THE BANNER INVIOLATE

Taken with reverence from the walls of the Keep Inviolate, this magnificent banner inspires all Knights of House Raven to greater glories. Those Nobles of House Raven who fight within sight of the banner feel the eyes of their ancestors upon them, and hear their whispered encouragements from the depths of their Thrones.

HOUSE RAVEN QUESTORIS CLASS model only. Re-roll hit rolls of 1 in the Fight phase for **HOUSE RAVEN** models whilst they are within 6" of the bearer.

FURY OF MARS

This remarkable weapon channels the fires of the Red Planet's hottest forges, eradicating its victims even at extreme range. It is said that to face the Fury of Mars is to be subjected to the killing ire of the Omnissiah himself, and to be struck down without mercy.

HOUSE TARANIS model with a thermal cannon only. Fury of Mars replaces the bearer's thermal cannon and has the following profile:

WEAPON	RANGE	TYPE	S	AP	D
Fury of Mars	48"	Heavy D6	9	-4	D6
Abilities: Roll two dice when inflicting damage with this weapon and discard the lowest result.					

THE HEADSMAN'S MARK

The Nobles of House Krast have a particular hatred for the traitorous Legio Mortis, and hunt down Chaos Titans wherever they get the chance. Those amongst their ranks who have struck the killing blow against such an enemy earn the right to bear the Headsman's Mark. More than just a badge of respect, this amulet feeds the pilot with targeting data that bolsters their giant-slaying skills still further.

HOUSE KRAST model only. Increase the Damage characteristic of the bearer's weapons by 1 for attacks made against enemy units containing models with a Wounds characteristic of 10 or more. Increase the Damage characteristic by 2 instead for attacks made against **TITANIC** units.

THE AURIC MASK

A massive upscaling of the eerie masks worn by the Nobles of House Vulker, this faceplate radiates terrifying contra-empathetic waves that spread panic and terror throughout the foe's ranks. Few can bear to even hold the gaze of the Knight suit that bears this mask, let alone stand defiant in battle against it.

HOUSE VULKER model only. The opposing player must roll an extra D6 when taking a Morale test for a unit within 12" of the bearer and use the highest result.

In the midst of fierce fighting on Ontoria XII, a Knight Crusader of House Taranis pauses to undergo repairs, rearm and refuel at a Sacristan Forgeshrine. A Tech-Priest Enginseer of the Adeptus Mechanicus oversees the works, his binharic prayers hastening and enhancing the auto-blessings imparted by the shrine.

FREEBLADE QUALITIES AND BURDENS

Whether they be fallen heroes, exiles seeking redemption, sole survivors or murderous lunatics, all Freeblade Knights possess traits and skills unique to themselves. For all their heroic qualities, these lonely warriors also carry terrible burdens, and it is these unusual martial facets – as much as their chosen panoply of war – that make each Freeblade distinct.

If your army is Battle-forged, then before the battle you can give one **Freeblade** model in each Detachment Qualities and Burdens. To do so, first either choose a single Quality from the table below, or roll two D6 to randomly generate two Qualities from the table (duplicate results have no effect). If your Battle-forged army includes Canis Rex, both **Canis Rex** and **Sir Hekhtur** have the Legendary Hero and Last of their Line Qualities.

D6 QUALITY
1. LAST OF THEIR LINE: *With no kin left to stand beside but many to avenge, this Freeblade fights outnumbered but never outgunned.*

Re-roll hit rolls of 1 for the Freeblade's attacks against units containing 10 or more models.

2. SWORN TO A QUEST: *Whether to fell a sworn nemesis or reclaim a powerful relic, this Freeblade's quest drives them ever onward.*

Re-roll hit rolls of 1 for this Freeblade when it targets the enemy Warlord. If this Freeblade is within range of an objective marker (as specified in the mission) it controls that objective marker even if there are more enemy models within range of the same objective marker. If an enemy unit within range of the same objective marker has a similar ability, then the objective marker is controlled by the player who has the most models within range of it as normal.

3. MYSTERIOUS GUARDIAN: *The Freeblade manifests as though from nowhere, an elemental force of vengeance against Mankind's foes.*

This Freeblade can perform Heroic Interventions as if it were a **Character**; it can do so if any enemy units are within 6" of it at the end of the enemy's charge phase, and can move up to 6" when doing so.

4. PEERLESS WARRIOR: *Through endless battle and practice, this Freeblade seeks to become the greatest of all Noble warriors.*

When this Quality is chosen or generated, roll a D6: on a 1-3 add 2" to this Freeblade's Move characteristic: on a 4-5 improve its Weapon Skill characteristic by 1 (e.g. WS3+ becomes WS2+); on a 6 improve its Ballistic Skill characteristic by 1 (e.g. BS3+ becomes BS2+).

5. INDOMITABLE: *This Freeblade is remarkable for their sheer resilience and bloody-minded determination.*

Add 1 to this Freeblade's Wounds and Leadership characteristics.

6. LEGENDARY HERO: *Tales of this Freeblade's exploits spread far and wide, and they are not exaggerations!*

Once per battle round, you can re-roll a single hit roll, wound roll, damage roll, charge roll or saving throw for this Freeblade.

After determining the model's Qualities, you must then either choose two different Burdens from the table below or roll one D6 to randomly generate a Burden. If your Battle-forged army includes Canis Rex, both **Canis Rex** and **Sir Hekhtur** have the Obsessed with Vengeance Burden.

If a Freeblade from your army has any Burdens, roll 2D6 for them at the start of each of your turns, subtracting 1 from the result if the Freeblade has the Exiled in Shame Burden. If the result is less than that Freeblade's Leadership characteristic, their Burdens do not apply that turn. If the result equals or exceeds their Leadership characteristic, then their Burdens apply until the start of your next turn.

D6 BURDEN
1. EXILED IN SHAME: *This Freeblade bears a mantle of ignominy and shame that they can never set aside.*

Whilst this Burden applies, the Freeblade cannot be affected by any Stratagems (this includes using the Command Re-roll Stratagem to re-roll a dice for this Freeblade).

2. WEARY MACHINE SPIRIT: *So long has this Freeblade fought that their Knight suit has become worn down in spirit and deed.*

Whilst this Burden applies, halve the number of wounds the Freeblade has remaining for the purposes of determining what characteristics to use on their damage table.

3. HAUNTED BY FAILURE: *Only once did this Freeblade fail, but the consequences mean they now constantly second-guess themselves.*

Whilst this Burden applies, re-roll hit rolls of 6 for the Freeblade.

4. OBSESSED WITH VENGEANCE: *This Freeblade's burning desire for retribution blinds them to all else.*

Whilst this Burden applies, the Freeblade can only target the nearest enemy unit that is visible to it in the Shooting phase, and it can only declare a charge against the nearest enemy unit in the Charge phase.

5. DRIVEN TO SLAUGHTER: *Blood-mad lunacy has consumed this Freeblade utterly. They are little more than wrath incarnate.*

Whilst this Burden applies, the Freeblade cannot Fall Back and its Ballistic Skill characteristic is changed to 6+.

6. IMPETUOUS NATURE: *This Freeblade's wild spirit leads them to make dangerous and irresponsible choices time and again.*

Whilst this Burden applies, every move that the Freeblade makes must take it closer to the nearest enemy model, and – unless it is already within 1" of an enemy unit – it must declare a charge against every enemy unit within 12" of it in your Charge phase.

POINTS VALUES

If you are playing a matched play game, or a game that uses a points limit, you can use the following lists to determine the total points cost of your army. Simply add together the points costs of all your models and the wargear they are equipped with to determine your army's total points value.

MELEE WEAPONS

WEAPON	POINTS PER WEAPON
Reaper chain-cleaver	0
Reaper chainsword	30
Thunderstrike gauntlet	35
Titanic feet	0

RANGED WEAPONS

WEAPON	POINTS PER WEAPON
Armiger autocannon	0
Avenger gatling cannon	75
Conflagration cannon	0
Heavy flamer	17
Heavy stubber	4
Ironstorm missile pod	16
Las-impulsor	0
Meltagun	17
Multi-laser	10
Plasma decimator	0
Rapid-fire battle cannon	100
Shieldbreaker missile	12
Stormspear rocket pod	45
Thermal cannon	76
Thermal spear	0
Thundercoil harpoon	0
Twin Icarus autocannon	30
Twin meltagun	0
Twin siegebreaker cannon	35
Volcano lance	0

UNITS

UNIT	MODELS PER UNIT	POINTS PER MODEL (Does not include wargear)
Armiger Helverin	1-3	170
Armiger Warglaive	1-3	160
Knight Castellan	1	510
Knight Crusader	1	285
Knight Errant	1	285
Knight Gallant	1	285
Knight Paladin	1	285
Knight Preceptor	1	385
Knight Valiant	1	500
Knight Warden	1	285
Sacristan Forgeshrine	1	80

NAMED CHARACTERS

UNIT	MODELS PER UNIT	POINTS PER MODEL (Including wargear)
Canis Rex	1	450

'Deeds of heroism and glory bring renown to your house, but zeal, faith and chivalry in the Omnissiah's name – these things will see your legacy last eternal.'

- Baron Dasorakis Gau-Taranis

TACTICAL OBJECTIVES

The tactics used by the Noble households combine their honourable approach to war with the unusual strategic facets of taking to the field entirely mounted in super-heavy war engines. Such methods of waging war have endured since the earliest days of the Knight worlds' founding, and have proved effective against innumerable xenos and heretic armies.

If your army is led by an **IMPERIAL KNIGHTS** Warlord, these Tactical Objectives replace the Capture and Control Tactical Objectives (numbers 11-16) in the *Warhammer 40,000* rulebook. If a mission uses Tactical Objectives, players use the normal rules for using Tactical Objectives with the following exception: when an Imperial Knights player generates a Capture and Control objective (numbers 11-16), they instead generate the corresponding Imperial Knights Tactical Objective, shown below. Other Tactical Objectives (numbers 21-66) are generated normally.

D66	TACTICAL OBJECTIVE
11	Yield No Ground
12	Duel of Honour
13	Assail the Foe
14	Titan Killer
15	Honour of the House
16	A Grudge to Settle

11 YIELD NO GROUND — *Imperial Knights*

The time has come to plant your feet and make a stand. For the glory of your house, take not one step back!

Score 1 victory point if there are no enemy units within your deployment zone at the end of your turn. Score D3 victory points instead if there are no enemy units within your deployment zone or within 12" of the centre of the battlefield at the end of your turn. This objective cannot be achieved on your first turn.

12 DUEL OF HONOUR — *Imperial Knights*

The foe is a dastardly coward, a cur that cannot be allowed to besmirch your honour much longer. Slay them with impunity.

Score 1 victory point if at least one enemy **CHARACTER** was destroyed in the Fight phase this turn by an **IMPERIAL KNIGHTS CHARACTER** from your army.

13 ASSAIL THE FOE — *Imperial Knights*

The savage joys of battle are upon you, surging through your systems, firing your blood. Attack! Attack!

Score 1 victory point if you made at least one successful charge with an **IMPERIAL KNIGHTS** unit this turn. If you made 3 or more successful charges with **IMPERIAL KNIGHTS** units this turn, score D3 victory points instead.

14 TITAN KILLER — *Imperial Knights*

The worthiest of foes is the mightiest! Only against such can you test your true mettle.

Score 1 victory point for each enemy **VEHICLE** or **MONSTER** model that was destroyed by an **IMPERIAL KNIGHTS** unit from your army this turn, and 3 victory points for each enemy **TITANIC** model that was destroyed by an **IMPERIAL KNIGHTS** unit from your army this turn, to a maximum of 6 victory points.

15 HONOUR OF THE HOUSE — *Imperial Knights*

It is unthinkable for an oath-sworn Noble to put their personal desires above the fealty they owe their household.

When this Tactical Objective is generated, your opponent must choose an **IMPERIAL KNIGHTS** unit from your army that is on the battlefield. Score 1 victory point if the chosen unit controls an objective marker at the end of two consecutive turns.

16 A GRUDGE TO SETTLE — *Imperial Knights*

The knightly households do not forget those who have deeply wronged them, and the vengeance of their Nobles can only be tempered in the blood of the hated foe.

When this Tactical Objective is generated, your opponent must nominate a unit from their army that is on the battlefield. Score 1 victory point if that unit was destroyed by an **IMPERIAL KNIGHTS** unit from your army this turn.

'TO SIT THE THRONE MECHANICUM, TO AWAKEN YOUR MANIFOLD AND FEEL YOUR KNIGHT COME TO LIFE AROUND YOU, THESE ARE THE STEPS OF A UNIQUE ASCENSION. YOUR SINEWS BECOME STEEL AND PISTONS. YOUR HEARTBEAT BECOMES PLASMIC FLAME. YOUR FISTS BECOME WEAPONS OF INCALCULABLE MIGHT. ALL SHALL FEAR YOU, AND WELL THEY SHOULD.'

- Canticles of the Precept to the Newly Become, Verses 35-37